VGM Opportunities Series

OPPORTUNITIES IN
FOOD SERVICE
CAREERS

Carol Ann Caprione Chmelynski

Foreword by
William P. Fisher, Ph.D.
Executive Vice President
National Restaurant Association

VGM Career Horizons
NTC/Contemporary Publishing Group

Library of Congress Cataloging-in-Publication Data

Chmelynski, Carol Ann Caprione, 1950–
    Opportunities in food service careers / Carol Ann Caprione
  Chmelynski ; foreword by William P. Fisher. — Rev. ed.
        p. cm. — (VGM opportunities series)
        ISBN 0-8442-3330-7 (c). — ISBN 0-8442-3407-9 (p)
        1. Food service—Vocational guidance. I. Title. II. Series.
  TX911.3.V62C45   1999
  647.95'023'73—dc21   99–38250
                                                               CIP

Cover photographs: © PhotoDisc, Inc.

Published by VGM Career Horizons
A division of NTC/Contemporary Publishing Group, Inc.
4255 West Touhy Avenue, Lincolnwood (Chicago), Illinois 60712-1975 U.S.A.
Printed in the United States of America.
International Standard Book Number: 0-8442-3330-7 (cloth)
                                          0-8442-3407-9 (paper)
 00 01 02 03 04 LB   19   18 17 16 15 14   13 12 11 10 9   8   7   6   5   4   3   2   1

CONTENTS

ABOUT THE AUTHOR

Carol Ann Caprione Chmelynski began her food service career in 1976 with the National Milk Producers Federation. She went on to become an editorial assistant at the Food Marketing Institute and later worked as a communications specialist at the National Restaurant Association in Washington, D.C., where she wrote feature articles for the association's monthly magazine, *NRA News.* That magazine is now titled *Restaurants USA.*

Ms. Chmelynski worked as a copywriter for the advertising firm of Stackig, Sanderson and White in McLean, Virginia, where she wrote product as well as job recruitment ads for high technology companies such as Electronic Data Systems, Network Solutions, Tempest Technologies, and Capital Systems Group, Inc.

Currently, Ms. Chmelynski is the assistant managing editor of *School Board News,* a biweekly newspaper of the National School Boards Association in Alexandria, Virginia.

ACKNOWLEDGMENTS

The author wishes to acknowledge the assistance of The Educational Foundation of the National Restaurant Association in Chicago, Illinois, and the National Restaurant Association in Washington, D.C., in the preparation of this book.

FOREWORD

By any measure the foodservice industry has enjoyed tremendous success over the past three decades, and the good news is that the projections for the future point to even greater growth as we begin the 21st century. The reasons for this favorable forecast are well known:

- a shift from a manufacturing based economy to a service based economy.
- more working women and more workers per household, including part-time, which causes more people to eat away from home, and pick up (or have delivered) food prepared away from home.
- a more active, mobile population.
- increasing personal disposable income of Americans, particularly those age 55 and above.

If you stop to think about all the places outside the home where food is prepared and/or served, you can begin to sense the size and the growth of the foodservice industry, and by extension, the growth of careers in foodservice. Not only do people eat meals in tablecloth restaurants, but they can also eat in fast-food establishments, coffee shops, cafeterias, in high schools and colleges, convention halls and sports stadiums, in recreation and amusement parks, on planes, in trains, in hospitals and nursing homes, in shopping malls and department stores, everywhere where people congregate. While many people eat more than 21 meals a week (seven days, three meals a days) nearly one-third to one-half, or more, are taken outside the home. And that trend is surging upward.

What an employment and a career opportunity! What an opportunity for growth in a growing industry! There has never been a better time for energetic, caring people to start on a foodservice career, and there are so many occupations from which to make a choice. You can work in the "heart of the house" such as the kitchen area, the "front of the house" such as the service area, or the "pulse of the house" such as the office. You can work for a large company or a small restaurant or anything in-between. The diversity is tremendous. There are no limits on your potential for growth and success in the foodservice industry. The opportunities abound! Go for them!

William P. Fisher, Ph.D.
Executive Vice President
National Restaurant Association

CHAPTER 1

AN OVERVIEW OF THE FOOD SERVICE INDUSTRY

The term "food service" applies to establishments that prepare food for consumption away from home. These food service establishments include:

- Restaurants of every kind: cafeterias, carryout operations, coffee shops, drugstore counters, fast-food chains, sandwich shops, and white tablecloth operations.
- Food preparation facilities in clubs, cocktail lounges, hotels, motels, and taverns.
- Airline, railroad, and steamship operations.
- Institutional food service, including school and college, hospital, industrial, military, and retirement home food service.

"Food service" also can be defined as opportunity and personal growth for qualified, enthusiastic, hardworking people.

THE LARGEST RETAIL EMPLOYER

Approximately 797,000 food service operations exist in the United States as of 1998. The food service industry prepares one-fifth of all food produced in the United States. That's 40 billion pounds of food, which is served during the course of nearly 200 million customer transactions each day.

Food service workers make up one of the largest and fastest growing occupational groups in the nation's labor force. More than three times as many people work in food service than in automobile manufacturing and steel manufacturing combined. In 1996, more than 10 million people were employed in food service. By the year 2006, the food service industry will need 2.3 million more people than it now employs. Food service opportunities will continue to expand because the number of working couples and singles is growing; this demographic factor means there will be an increased demand for food prepared away from home. Job opportunities exist almost everywhere and for almost any interested person, including those who have limited skills or little formal education.

GROWTH OF THE INDUSTRY

The food service industry is truly a growing one. In 1973, there were 490,000 establishments. In 1977, that number increased to 535,000. In 1982, 559,000. In 1991, 657,000. Consumers are spending a growing proportion of their food dollar away from home: 33.6 percent in 1972, 37 percent in 1979, and 43 percent in 1991. Food service industry sales increased dramatically in the 1970s, rising from $42.8 billion in 1970 to $119.6 billion in 1980. In 1988, industry sales were $211.8 billion. In 1991, food service sales were 248.1 billion. In 1999, food service sales are projected to be $354 billion.

INDUSTRY DIVERSITY

There are many ways to define the components of the food service industry. Beginning with the concept that the industry provides all meals, snacks, and drinks prepared outside the home, it is considered to have three main branches: commercial, institutional, and military feeding.

Commercial Feeding

The commercial feeding group comprises those establishments that are open to the public, are operated for profit, and that may operate facilities and/or supply meal service on a regular basis for others. Commercial feeding accounts for nearly 74 percent of industry sales, and includes restaurants, food service contractors, hotel and motel restaurants, and restaurants in department stores, drugstores, and so forth.

Some of the different types of commercial feeding establishments are:

Family-type restaurant. This is a restaurant one would be inclined to frequent with family, spouse, or friends for a casual meal. The atmosphere is likely to be relaxed and unpretentious, featuring fast service. Reservations, in most cases, are not necessary. This kind of operation is well known and the most used, especially during meal hours.

Atmosphere restaurant. This is the type of restaurant that creates an atmosphere by virtue of setting, decor, historic context, special artifacts, or view. Although you might take your family, you would probably have a special reason for patronizing this type of restaurant. One would be likely to dress better when going to an atmosphere restaurant than when patronizing a family restaurant.

Gourmet restaurant. One would patronize this type of restaurant because the food, service, and gracious atmosphere contribute to a relaxed dining experience. It is more formal than the family or atmosphere restaurant, and it is characterized by an unhurried pace. This type of restaurant might be selected for a special occasion or because good food and service on a particular dining-out occasion are sought.

Fast-Food restaurant. This type of restaurant primarily sells limited refreshments and prepared food items, such as fish, hamburger, chicken, or roast beef sandwiches for consumption either on or near the premises or for take-home consumption. In recent years, fast-food restaurants have added such items as desserts and salads to their menu. This type of restaurant is inexpensive, appeals to all ages, and is suitable for snack service as well as meal service. Seating is available, but customers may order and pick up the food at the counter. Fast-food restaurants are primarily chain or franchise units.

Cafeterias. These feeding establishments serve prepared food and beverages, usually through a cafeteria line where customers make selections from a wide display of items. Some limited waiter or waitress service may be provided. Table and/or booth seating facilities are usually provided. Cost is usually low to moderate.

Take-out restaurant. This type of restaurant's primary interest is food taken off the premises. No seating is available. It is inexpensive to moderate in price and may involve home delivery.

The types of commercial feeding establishments listed above are to some extent arbitrary, and restaurant categories rarely have neat, sharp boundaries.

Institutional Feeding

The institutional feeding group is comprised of business, educational, government, and institutional organizations that operate

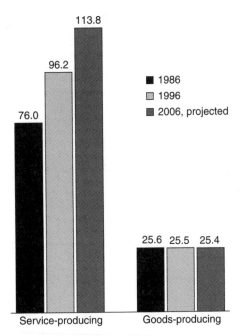

**Wage and salary employment by industry
sector, 1986, 1996, and projected 2006**
(millions)

Source: United States Department of Labor, Bureau of Labor Statistics

their own food services. Food is provided as an auxiliary service
necessary to support their other activities. Although some establishments operate for profit, this is not the aim of the institutional
food service activity. Rather, such institutions serve food princi-
pally as a convenience for their own employees, students, patients,
etc. In 1995, there were 176,000 institutional feeding units in the
United States.

Military Feeding

Military feeding comprises the sale of food and beverages at officers' and enlisted persons' clubs and military exchanges, as well as food service to troops in a defense capacity. In 1991, there were 1,000 military feeding units in the nation.

CHAPTER 2

FOOD SERVICE
CAREER OPPORTUNITIES

A position in the food service industry offers exciting prospects for growth and personal satisfaction in helping to meet one of society's basic needs—the need for food.

The food service industry is the primary retail employer in the United States. Over 10 million people have found their careers in food service. Each year, more than 300,000 new employees will be needed to supply the growing demand for the industry's services. Through good economic times and bad, this growth has remained steady, making a career in food service a career with a future.

Food service offers good potential to people at all levels of educational attainment. Almost any interested person, including people who have limited skills or little formal education, can find a niche in the food service industry. To the high school graduate, a career in food service is an immediate possibility. Advanced academic training in junior and community colleges or in four-year college or university programs greatly expands career potential.

The food service industry provides opportunities for people of virtually all ages. For sixteen-year-old high school students, or for those who are beginning or changing a career later in life, a career with the food service industry can be an excellent choice.

A VARIETY OF JOBS AND CAREERS

Careers in the food service industry are many and varied. There are no formal educational requirements for many food service jobs, and skills are usually learned through on-the-job training. Many restaurants hire inexperienced people as dining room attendants, sanitation/maintenance workers, counter workers, waiters, waitresses, and bartenders. However, experience sometimes is necessary to obtain one of these positions in a large restaurant or catering firm. Previous employment in a food service occupation, such as kitchen helper or assistant cook, often is necessary to secure a job as a cook. Experienced workers may advance to food service manager, maitre d'hôtel, head waiter, or chef. Top-level positions usually require academic training and on-the-job experience. The amount of career preparation determines the entry level into the food service field. The depth as well as the breadth of the field guarantees ample room for upward movement by those entering it.

Vocational schools, both public and private, offer courses in cooking, catering, and bartending. Employment of food service workers is expected to increase faster than the average for all occupations through 2006. The demand for these workers will increase as new restaurants, cafeterias, and bars open in response to population growth and increased spending for food and beverages outside the home. Higher average incomes and more leisure time will allow people to eat out more often. Also, as more women join the work force, families are finding dining out a welcome convenience. In addition to growth in demand for these workers, thousands of job openings will occur each year from high turnover, especially from students working part-time. Details concerning the work, training, outlook, and earning of employees are discussed in Chapters 7, 8, and 9.

Entry-Level Positions

Food service entry-level positions usually require a minimum of training. Dining room attendants include the positions of bus person, hat checker, food server, host, hostess, sanitation/maintenance worker, and bartender's helper.

A brief description of these entry-level positions follows. For a more detailed look at general dining room attendants and dishwashers, see Chapter 7.

Bus person. Bus persons clear and reset dining tables with fresh linen and silverware. They refill water glasses, and assist waiters and waitresses in serving and housekeeping chores in the dining area. A job as bus person provides an excellent way to start acquiring food service expertise.

Hat checker. Hat checkers are responsible for guarding coats, hats, briefcases, and other personal articles that customers do not want in their immediate possession while dining.

Host, hostess. Hosts and hostesses maintain reservation lists, greet customers, show guests to tables, ensure order and cleanliness in the dining area, and, in some cases, may handle complaints. This job requires good organization skills, tact, a ready smile, neat appearance, and an affinity for people.

Food server. Food servers, commonly known as waiters and waitresses, are responsible for food orders and service to customers. Food servers must like people and be poised and efficient under the stress of simultaneous demands. Many energetic, outgoing people make this their career.

Sanitation/maintenance worker. Sanitation/maintenance workers ensure that walls and floors are clean and that there is a steady supply of clean cooking equipment, utensils, dishware, and silver. Most modern food service operations have dishwashers and other machines to assist in speeding these tasks. Good sanitation and maintenance are vital to any food service operation.

Bartender's helper. Bartender's helpers assist the bartender in maintaining bar stock, cleaning glassware, replenishing supplies of ice, and cleaning the bar area. This job offers excellent background for becoming a bartender.

Middle-Level Positions

Bartender. A bartender requires an excellent memory for hundreds of beverages ranging from the common to the exotic. Bartenders both serve customers and fill drink orders taken by food servers. A congenial personality and knowledge of how to order for and stock the bar, as well as maintain inventories of liquor and glassware, is needed. Also, bartenders must be familiar with state and local laws concerning sale of alcoholic beverages.

Cashier. The cashier receives payment from customers, so good mathematical skills are necessary. Because she or he is a customer-contact person, the cashier must be tactful, friendly, and gracious.

Food checker. The food checker is responsible for verifying each food order as it leaves the kitchen.

Cook. Cooks prepare food for eating

Chef. Although the term *chef* and *cook* are often used interchangeably, the professional chef is generally a far more skilled, trained, and experienced person. Chefs, sometimes referred to as head cooks, coordinate the work of the kitchen staff and often direct certain kinds of food preparation. They decide the size of the serving, sometimes plan menus, and buy food supplies. The positions of chef and cook can be highly creative ones. In large operations, the positions are often specialized with one or more individuals responsible for specific product categories such as vegetables, soups, meats, or sauces.

Pastry chef, baker. The pastry chef or baker is responsible for the desserts. This includes baking cakes, cookies, pies, bread, rolls, and quick breads. Sometimes skill in cake decoration is also required.

Pantry Supervisor. The pantry supervisor is responsible for supervising salad, sandwich, and beverage workers, and also should be able to create attractive food arrangements. The supervision of cleaning crews and responsibility for supply requisition may also be part of the job.

Dining room manager. The position of dining room manager requires an objective, fair, conscientious, and observant leader. Dining room managers supervise all dining room staff and activities, including staff training, scheduling of staff working hours, keeping time records, and assigning work stations. These managers should be capable of working in a formal public atmosphere. They are sometimes known as waiter-captain, head waitress, or food service supervisor.

Purchasing agent/storeroom supervisor. The purchasing agent/storeroom supervisor orders, receives, inspects, and stores all goods shipped by suppliers and oversees distribution to different food preparation departments. Requirements include inventory management skill, knowledge of good food storage practices, and up-to-date knowledge of market prices. Sometimes these duties are assigned to the manager or chef.

Meatcutter. Meatcutters must be expertly skilled in cutting down beef, veal, lamb, and pork from full, half, or quarter carcasses to serving portions which are cut, trimmed, and prepared to the chef's orders. Cutting poultry and seafood also may be one of the duties.

INDUSTRY GROWTH POTENTIAL

Food service is a growing and thriving industry. According to new Bureau of Labor Statistics (BLS) employment projections, employment growth in the food service industry will outpace that for most other industries through 2006.

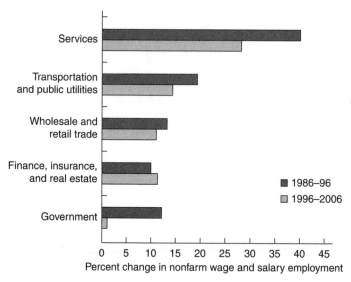

Percent change in employment in service-producing industries, 1986–96 and projected 1996–2006

Source: United States Department of Labor, Bureau of Labor Statistics

Employment in service-producing industries will increase faster than average, with growth near 30 percent. The strong job growth potential projected for the food service industry is the result of several factors:

- unit expansion in the industry, particularly the fast-food segment;
- the aging of the U.S. population;
- an increase in one- and two-person households; and
- a continued increase in the number of working women.

All of the above-mentioned demographic trends are expected to increase the number of people eating out, thus creating a demand for more workers to serve restaurant patrons in coming years.

CHAPTER 3

JOB TRAINING AND QUALIFICATIONS

CAREER LADDERS

The food service industry is now, more than ever, interested in training and retraining personnel who are qualified for food service careers, motivated to perform, and interested in staying on the job. More and more food service operations have implemented a career development system to assure their personnel that there are no dead-end jobs in food service. On-the-job training that will provide restaurant employees with a systematic and visible way of moving upward is a key concern of restaurant operators. This sequence of jobs through which food service employees can be promoted is commonly referred to as a *career ladder.*

Career ladders link together jobs that use similar skills and knowledge, thus providing opportunities for upward movement of employees within one department. While new skills and knowledge are added at each upward step, each job should be seen by the employee as preparation for something better and more challenging.

A simple example of a career ladder might be someone hired as short-order cook, who is then promoted to kitchen helper, cook, executive cook, and finally, chef. Of course, sometimes it may be necessary to change the place of employment to achieve higher positions. Keep in mind that many of the food service skills are interrelated, and the opportunity to learn new skills should never be neglected by the employee with a far-reaching career goal in mind.

OPPORTUNITIES FOR WOMEN AND MINORITIES

Women and minorities are well represented in all job categories throughout the food service industry, and their share of these jobs is steadily on the increase.

The U.S. Department of Labor, Bureau of Labor Statistics reports employment of African-Americans and Hispanics in food service is climbing at twice the twenty-seven percent rate for all industries combined. The food service industry employs more women and minorities as managers than any other industry. Many restaurant chains even offer special training programs for new women and minority employees and provide role models to guide them in their careers.

FOOD SERVICE MANAGEMENT POSITIONS

Experience and education are two attributes that usually are required for qualification for higher-level management positions in the food service industry.

Restaurant manager. Managers are responsible for efficiency, quality, and courtesy in all phases of a food service operation. In large organizations, the managers may direct supervisory personnel at the next lower level. In smaller operations, they might supervise kitchen and dining room staffs directly. A thorough knowledge of the responsibilities of all restaurant staff is necessary in this position.

Assistant manager. Assistant managers perform specialized supervisory duties under the manager's direction. They must be capable of filling in when the manager is absent, and thus must have good management skills and familiarity with overall food service operations.

Food production manager. This position entails responsibility for all food preparation and supervision of kitchen staff. Workers must possess leadership skills and have knowledge of food preparation techniques, quality and sanitation standards, and cost-control methods.

Personnel director. Personnel directors usually are employed in larger restaurants, food service chains, or as specialists in hotel or institutional food service operations. Personnel directors are responsible for hiring and training food service personnel and for administering employee relations, benefits, safety, and communications programs.

Menu planner. Menu planners select all food items offered on menus. They must know food service costs, preparation techniques and equipment, and consumer trends and preferences. This position usually requires a college or associate degree in dietetics or foods and nutrition. Restaurant managers, food production managers, or chefs may have these responsibilities assigned to them.

Merchandising supervisor. Merchandising supervisors plan and carry out advertising and promotional programs to increase sales. Creativity and the knowledge required to work with printers, artists, writers, and other suppliers are necessary. In addition, they must know their employer's food service operation thoroughly, be able to apply market research techniques, and be skilled in budgeting and planning. This position usually requires a college degree in advertising, marketing, merchandising, or a related field.

Director of recipe development. This director creates new recipes for the menus of larger restaurants or restaurant chains. Thorough knowledge of food preparation and the ability to apply this knowledge creatively are required.

PERSONALITY TRAITS

Food service is a "people" business. A pleasing personality is crucial to success in this field. Meeting and working with people is the nature of the industry, so a food service worker must possess the qualities that other people like to deal with including:

- friendliness
- diplomacy
- helpfulness
- attentiveness
- humor
- sympathy
- enthusiasm
- creativity

People who do well in food service careers possess a combination of human qualities that contribute to their advancement in the field.

WORK ATTITUDES

There is no substitute for positive work attitudes, which include the following basics:

- punctuality
- pride in personal appearance
- businesslike manner

- eagerness to learn
- willingness to work
- ability to accept criticism and direction

The food service industry has a need and a place for people at all job levels. Opportunities to gain experience and on-the-job, as well as academic, training are excellent. However, the ambition to use these opportunities as stepping stones to advancement is a vital attribute.

ABILITY TO HANDLE STRESS

Because every food service operation involves peak periods and deadlines leading up to them, pressures can be intense. A healthy mental outlook that enables individuals to function well with fellow workers while serving the public effectively is a must. Good physical condition is also necessary, because much of the time is spent on your feet and lifting heavy items.

The major goal of every food service operation is the satisfaction of the food service customer. The people who choose to work in the industry must recognize this goal and dedicate themselves to its achievement.

A career in food service is a demanding one, but it can provide many rewards. If you enjoy meeting, working with, and serving people, this business is suited to you.

CHAPTER 4

SALARIES AND BENEFITS

SALARIES

According to figures from the U.S. Department of Labor, Bureau of Statistics data, 1996 salaries for certain food service occupations were as follows:

	Mean Wage	
	Hourly	*Annual*
Bartender	$6.70	$13,940*
Food counter workers	$6.42	$13,360*
Waiters/waitresses	$5.87	$12,200*
Dining room attendants	$6.26	$13,020**
Cooks, restaurant	$8.06	$16,770
institution or cafeteria	$8.02	$16,670
fast food	$6.11	$12,700
short order	$7.16	$14,900
Meatcutters	$11.24	$23,370

*Tips usually average between 10 and 20 percent of patrons' checks.

**These employees may receive a percentage of waiters' and waitresses' tips.

The benefits for someone considering a career in the food service industry are substantial. Because the industry needs more

19

than 300,000 new employees each year, the competition for enthusiastic, highly motivated, career-minded people is high. There are increased wage scales from entry-level positions to top-level management jobs. Salaries in the food service industry are highly comparable to other industries.

ADDITIONAL BENEFITS

Salary is not the only area where the food service industry is competitive with other industries. Many extra benefits also are available. Of course, they vary from company to company, but included among the fringe benefits of the food service industry are:

- meals
- uniforms
- paid vacation
- paid holidays
- paid sick leave
- other miscellaneous leave with pay
- medical plans
- dental plans
- group life insurance
- accidental death and dismemberment insurance
- profit sharing/thrift savings plan
- pension plan
- stock purchase
- education assistance

FOOD SERVICE CAREER FLEXIBILITY

Location

The food service industry offers employment in every city and town in the country. The pay scale for many jobs is higher in the larger metropolitan cities than in smaller towns, but jobs are available everywhere.

Hours

Because restaurants are open from early in the morning to late at night, and some are even open all night, a job in food service can meet anyone's schedule needs. The flexibility of the hours are especially appealing to students, young parents, and anyone who desires part-time work.

Work Styles

A career in food service can mean a secure job with little responsibility, or a job with a great deal of responsibility.

In food service, there is a place for people to lead others with their creativity, supervisory, and management skills, or there is a place for those who prefer to follow such leaders. The food service industry truly offers something for everyone's needs. It is possible to start in some jobs with no previous experience or training, and learn on the job. Following this, a person can take day or nighttime classes in many different kinds of food service skills if they wish to progress.

Community and junior colleges, trade schools, culinary institutes, and four-year colleges offer a great variety of training possibilities to choose from. It is also a fact that people can still get training on the job in food services, and with hard work and an aptitude for business, they eventually can become owners or managers of an operation.

CHAPTER 5

EDUCATIONAL REQUIREMENTS

HIGH SCHOOL OPPORTUNITIES

The more training and education an individual has, the better the opportunity to begin employment at a higher level of income and responsibility. In the food service industry, however, no one has to drop out of the running for lack of training or education. More than in many other industries, entry-level career opportunities exist in great variety. The ambitious, hard-working, and career-minded individual can find a route to the top in this industry. Thus a career in food service is well worth considering by the recent high school graduate who plans an immediate career start. It's also ideal for the individual who wishes to begin or change a career later in life.

Most food service operations are willing to invest time and money in training newcomers to the field. Once a person has gained a sound base of knowledge, it is possible to move upward into jobs with more responsibility and better pay.

Students still in school can accelerate their food service career development by taking food service courses offered in high schools or vocational schools. Depending on the type and number of courses taken, these can give the graduate a slight advantage when seeking employment. Also, part-time work in a food service job while still in school can be a valuable aid.

JUNIOR AND COMMUNITY COLLEGES

One of the richest sources of new management talent in the food service industry is found in junior and community colleges that offer associate degrees in various aspects of food service. Hundreds of jobs are open to graduates with this training.

Two-year college programs pave the way for graduates to undertake a variety of beginning administrative and supervisory jobs in many types of food service operations.

Some of the courses available at junior and community colleges include:

- food purchasing and storage
- food preparation
- menu planning
- equipment purchasing and layout
- personnel management and job analysis
- food standards and sanitation
- diet therapy
- catering
- beverage control
- food cost accounting
- recordkeeping

In addition to the above, a number of general courses, designed to broaden the student's knowledge and outlook, may include the following:

- communication skills
- psychology
- sociology

- economics
- chemistry
- nutrition
- physical education

Many community and junior college programs are less expensive than other college programs, and they combine classroom work with practical job experience in part-time food service jobs. Many food service operators support their local college programs by providing part-time employment for students and also career opportunities for graduates. (See Appendix D for a list of community and junior colleges that offer programs concerned with hotel, restaurant, and institutional management.)

FOUR-YEAR UNIVERSITIES OR COLLEGES

The food service industry's need for graduates of four-year college programs in management has never really been filled. Numerous management and management training positions are open in all segments of the industry including:

- assistant manager
- food production supervisor
- purchasing agent
- food cost accountant
- food service director
- director of recipe development
- sales manager
- banquet manager

Jobs are offered in all types of organizations including restaurant chain operations, institutional food service, club management, and airline in-flight catering.

Undergraduate programs include:

- basic and advanced courses in food preparation
- specialized courses in restaurant accounting, catering, management, and sanitation
- general courses in economics, law, marketing, cost control, and finance

A requirement of many four-year colleges includes summer work in hotels, restaurants, and institutions. Graduates of four-year programs receive bachelor's degrees in the following:

- restaurant or institutional management
- dietetics
- home economics
- business administration

See Appendix E for a list of college programs in hotel, restaurant, and institutional management.

An ever-increasing number of colleges and universities are also offering master's and doctoral degree programs in food service administration and restaurant and hotel management.

There are literally thousands of choices of schools of different kinds in the food service industries, and more are continually being developed. An extensive list is included at the end of this book. In addition, when you are ready to select a school, you should contact the school authorities in your area, write to the sources they suggest, and visit as many schools as you need in order to develop an understanding of the choices available to you.

After you have investigated the possibilities, it is a good idea to discuss them with people in the field or career guidance counselors who can help you to evaluate your choices.

CHAPTER 6

FINANCIAL AID

SCHOLARSHIPS, GRANTS, AND FELLOWSHIPS

The Educational Foundation of the National Restaurant Association makes a number of scholarships available to students of food service management, including hotel-restaurant management, institutional management, dietetics, culinary arts, nutrition, food marketing, food science, and other food service curricula.

To be eligible for scholarships, students are required to have full-time status for the full academic year beginning with the fall term, be enrolled in a food service hospitality-related curriculum full time, and be pursuing an associate, bachelor's, or master's degree.

Judging for these scholarships is based on:

- industry work experience
- academic standing
- views on the industry

For the 1999–2000 school year, more than $600,000 in scholarships will be awarded. One hundred awards ranging in value from $1,000 to $10,000, as well as one $2,000 award, will be awarded to high school seniors, undergraduate college students, and graduate students. The grants are for one year only. There is no automatic right of continuance; applicants must reapply each year. The scholarship award may be applied toward tuition, fees, books, supplies, and other educational necessities.

Eligibility requirements demand that each applicant be enrolled in or plan to enroll in a formally accredited academic curriculum in which food service is a basic component, in pursuit of the customary degree showing successful accomplishment of the program. Such programs include, but are not limited to, hospitality management, culinary arts, dietetics, nutrition, food marketing, food science, and distribution.

To be considered for a scholarship award, applicants must complete and send an application form, along with a transcript of the their grades demonstrating one complete year of study prior to application, to the Educational Foundation of the National Restaurant Association. The address is:

The Educational Foundation of the National Restaurant Association
    The Scholarship Department
    250 S. Wacker Drive, Suite 1400
    Chicago, IL 60606
    (312) 715-1010
    (800) 765-2122

Applications are available January 1; the deadline for application is March 1. (For graduate students applications are available November 1; deadline for application is February 15.)

Selection of award recipients will be made in May during the annual National Restaurant Association show ny the scholarship committee, which is composed of educators and industry members.

Teacher Work Study Grants

In the upcoming scholastic year, 8 NRA-NIFI Teacher Work-Study Grants, each in the amount of $3,000 will be awarded on a competitive basis to teachers and administrators of food service career education programs. These awards are made possible by a grant from the National Restaurant Association and will be administered by The Educational Foundation. The grants give recipients the chance to obtain work experience in the food service industry that will enrich and update their knowledge of the industry and thus increase their capability to impart that knowledge to their students.

Arrangements for work-study employment should be made by each applicant. Recipients of these grants must be paid by the employer at a rate commensurate with the position. The grant funds are intended to supplement money earned during employment.

To be considered by the scholarship committee, an applicant must:

- Give specific and complete answers to all questions. If a question does not apply to the applicant, answer using the letters N/A (not applicable).
- Be supported by a letter of recommendation from her/his immediate supervisor.
- Arrange for eight consecutive weeks of employment, an average of 40 hours each week, totaling a minimum of 320 hours within this eight-week period.
- Obtain a letter from her/his prospective employer who indicates a willingness to employ the applicant as proposed above.
- Be committed to continue teaching full-time in a hotel-restaurant-institutional food service program at an educational institution, or attend school full-time pursuing an advanced degree for the upcoming academic year.

Selection of winners will be made by an independent scholarship committee composed of educators and leaders of the industry.

Application forms are available November 1 directly from the Educational Foundation. The deadline for application is February 15.

H. J. Heinz Graduate Fellowships

The H.J. Heinz graduate degree fellowships are awarded on a competitive basis to teachers and administrators enrolled in academic programs leading to a master's degree or doctoral degree to improve their skills in teaching food service courses or administering food service career education.

There are seven fellowships in all: $1,000–$2,000 (maximum) fellowships per academic year.

Individuals interested in growing professionally and increasing their capability to relate knowledge to students are encouraged to apply. Application forms are available October 1 from the Educational Foundation; the deadline for application is December 31.

Selection of award recipients will be made in May during the annual National Restaurant Association show by the scholarship committee, which is composed of educators and industry members.

CHAPTER 7

ENTRY-LEVEL POSITIONS

An egg-stained fork, a soiled tablecloth, or an empty salt shaker can make a customer very unhappy and may damage a restaurant's reputation. Dining room attendants and sanitation/maintenance workers provide the quick hands and sharp eyes needed to prevent such problems.

Entry-level positions in the food service industry are often looked upon as jobs so easy that almost anyone can do them. Waiting on tables, making salads, and taking care of the soda fountain are, nevertheless, positions of responsibility.

DINING ROOM ATTENDANTS

Dining room attendants perform many tasks that otherwise food servers would be responsible for. They clear and reset tables, carry soiled dishes to the dishwashing area, bring in trays of food, and clean up spilled food and broken dishes. By handling these details, attendants give waiters and waitresses more time to serve customers. In some restaurants, attendants help food servers by serving water and bread and butter to customers. Also, when business is slow, they handle various jobs such as refilling salt and pepper shakers and cleaning coffee pots.

SANITATION/MAINTENANCE WORKERS

Sanitation/maintenance workers (dishwashers) continue where dining room attendants leave off. They are responsible for operating special machines that clean tableware quickly and efficiently. To keep machines in optimum operating order, dishwashers may have to make minor adjustments to their machines.

Sanitation/maintenance workers may clean large pots and pans by hand or operate a mechanical pot-and-pan washer. In addition, they may clean refrigerators and other kitchen equipment, sweep and mop floors, and carry out trash.

Working Conditions

Many dining room attendants and sanitation/maintenance workers work less than thirty hours a week. Some are on duty only a few hours a day during either the lunch or dinner period. Others work both periods but take a few hours off in the middle of the day. Weekend and holiday work is often a requirement.

Job injuries are seldom serious, but hazards do include the possibility of falls, cuts, and burns. The work is considered strenuous, because the workers are required to lift heavy trays filled with dishes and large pots and pans.

Places of Employment

Most dining room attendants and sanitation/maintenance workers are employed in restaurants, bars, and hotels. Sanitation/maintenance workers also work in schools, hospitals, and other institutional feeding operations.

Training, Other Qualifications, and Advancement

To qualify for jobs as dining room attendants and sanitation/maintenance workers, a high school education is not needed.

Many employers will hire applicants who do not speak English. Workers must be in good physical condition and have physical stamina because they stand most of the time, lift and carry trays, and work at a fast pace during busy periods. State laws often require these employees to obtain health certificates to show that they are free of contagious diseases. Because of their close contact with people, attendants should be neat in appearance, maintain good personal hygiene, and get along well with people.

Promotions for dining room attendants and sanitation/maintenance workers are available. Attendants often advance to positions as food servers, and sanitation/maintenance workers may advance to the position of cook's helper or short-order cook. In order to obtain a promotion of this type, the ability to read, write, and do simple arithmetic is required. Opportunities for advancement are most often found in large restaurants.

Employment Outlook

Job openings for dining room attendants and sanitation/maintenance workers are expected to be plentiful in the coming years. Many openings will come about from the need to replace workers who find jobs in other occupations, retire, or die. Among parttime workers, turnover is particularly high. Approximately fifty percent of dining room attendants and sanitation/maintenance workers are students who work part time while attending school.

Employment growth will provide additional openings. Jobs for dining room attendants and sanitation/maintenance workers are expected to increase faster than the average for all occupations through the year 2006 as population growth and higher incomes create more business for those engaged in food service establishments.

Earnings

Dining room attendants and sanitation/maintenance workers have relatively low earnings. Median weekly earnings were about $260 in 1996. The middle 50 percent earned between $200 and $320; the top 10 percent earned over $410 a week. Most received over half of their earnings as wages; the rest of their income was their share of the proceeds from tip pools. These amounts fell below the average earnings of most other supervisory workers in private industry, with the exception of those in farming. In establishments covered by federal law, workers beginning at the minimum wage earn $5.15 an hour.

Many employers furnish dining room attendants and sanitation/maintenance workers with uniforms and free meals. In addition, paid vacations and various types of health insurance and pension plans are included in their overall employee benefit plan.

The principal union organizing dining room assistants and sanitation/maintenance workers is the Hotel Employees and Restaurant Employees International Union (AFL-CIO).

Related Occupations

Other food service-related jobs that require little formal education but provide comfort and convenience to workers are bell captains, building custodians, hospital attendants, and porters.

FOOD SERVERS

All food servers, commonly known as waiters and waitresses, have essentially the same job. Whether they work in small lunchrooms or fashionable restaurants, food servers take customers' orders, serve food and beverages, make out checks, and sometimes take payments. The way in which food servers perform their duties may vary considerably, however. In coffee shops, diners, and other small restaurants, food servers are expected to provide fast, efficient service. In eating establishments where meals are served elaborately and a great deal of emphasis is placed on the satisfaction and comfort of each guest, food servers serve food at a more leisurely pace and offer more personal service to their patrons. As an example, they may suggest wines and explain the preparation of items on the menu.

Food servers often perform duties other than waiting on tables. These additional tasks may include setting up tables and clearing and carrying soiled flatware to the kitchen. Although very small restaurants usually combine waiting on tables with counter service or cashiering, larger or more formal restaurants frequently relieve their food servers of these additional duties.

Many food servers work split shifts, which means they work for several hours during the day, take a few hours off in the afternoon, and return to their jobs for the evening hours. Most are required to work on holidays and weekends. The wide range in dining hours creates a good opportunity for part-time work.

In considering the career, however, remember that food servers stand most of the time and often carry heavy trays of food. During peak dining hours, they may need to rush to several tables at once. Although the work is relatively safe, they must be careful to avoid slips, falls, and burns.

Places of Employment

Approximately 2 million food servers were employed in 1996. More than fifty percent worked part time (less than thirty-five hours a week). The majority worked in restaurants; some worked in hotels, motels, colleges, and factories which have restaurant facilities. Jobs are located throughout the country but are most plentiful in large cities and tourist areas. Seasonal employment can be found in vacation resorts. Some food servers alternate between summer and winter resorts instead of remaining in one area the entire year.

Training, Other Qualifications, and Advancement

An applicant who has had at least two or three years of high school is most preferred by employers. A person may start as a food server, or advance to that position after working as a dining room attendant, carhop, or food counter worker. Although most food servers obtain their skill through on-the-job training, at least three months experience is preferred by larger restaurants and hotels. Some private and public vocational schools, restaurant associations, and large restaurant chains provide classroom training. Other employers use self-instruction programs to train new employees. In these programs, a worker learns food preparation and service skills by observing film strips and reading instructional booklets on the subject.

Close and constant contact with the public makes a neat appearance and even disposition important qualifications for this occupation. Physical stamina is important, because food servers are on their feet for hours at a time, lifting and carrying trays of food from kitchen to dining table. Food servers also should have good mathematical skills. In restaurants specializing in foreign foods where some patrons may not speak English, knowledge of a foreign language is helpful. State laws often require food servers to obtain health certificates stating they are free of contagious diseases.

Because most food serving establishments are small, opportunities for promotion in this area may be limited. However, after gaining some experience, a food server may transfer to a larger restaurant where earnings and prospects for advancement are better. Successful food servers are those who genuinely like people, offer good service, and possess the ability to sell rather than just take orders. Advancement can be to cashier or to supervisory jobs, such as maitre d'hôtel or dining room supervisor. Some supervisory workers advance to jobs as restaurant managers.

Employment Outlook

In the years ahead, job opportunities are expected to be plentiful. This is mainly due to the need to replace the food servers who find other jobs, retire, die, or stop working for other reasons. Turnover is especially high among part-time workers. Approximately twenty-five percent of the food servers are students, most of whom work part time while attending school and then find other jobs after graduation. Many job openings also will result from employment growth.

Employment of food servers is expected to increase about as fast as the average for all occupations through the year 2006, as population growth and higher incomes create more business for food service operations. More leisure time and higher incomes will permit people to eat out more often. In addition, as more women join the work force, families may find dining out a welcome convenience.

The best employment opportunities for beginning food servers will be found in the thousands of informal restaurants. Those seeking jobs in expensive restaurants may find keen competition for the jobs that become available.

Earnings

According to the Department of Labor, median weekly earnings for food servers in 1996 (for full-time servers) were about $270. The middle 50 percent earned between $200 and $350; the top ten percent earned at least $470 a week. It must be remembered, however, that for many food servers, tips are greater than hourly wages. Tips generally average between 10 and 20 percent of guests' checks. Most food servers receive meals at work, and many are furnished with uniforms.

The principal union organizing food servers is the Hotel and Restaurant Employees and Bartenders International Union (AFL-CIO).

Related Occupations

Other occupations that involve serving customers and helping them feel at ease and enjoy themselves include flight attendants, butlers, counter workers, hosts and hostesses, and bellhops.

FOOD COUNTER WORKERS

Counter workers serve customers in eating places that specialize in fast service and inexpensive food, such as hamburger and fried chicken carryouts, drugstore soda fountains, and school and public cafeterias. Based on the Bureau of the Census survey, more than 1.7 million persons, most of whom worked part time, had food counter jobs in 1996. Accuracy in handling orders and speed of service are the most important job skills for food counter workers. Typical duties include taking customers' orders, serving food and beverages, making out checks, and taking payments. At drugstore fountains and in diners, cooking, making sandwiches, preparing cold drinks, and making sundaes also are part of food-counter workers' duties. Where food is prepared in an assembly-line manner, as in hamburger carryouts, counter workers may take turns waiting on customers, making french fries, toasting buns, and doing other jobs.

In cafeterias, counter workers supply serving lines with desserts, salads, and other dishes, in addition to filling customers' plates with meats and side orders. Usually central cashiers are employed by cafeterias to take payments and make change.

Counter workers also are responsible for odd jobs, such as cleaning kitchen equipment, sweeping and mopping floors, and carrying out trash.

Working Conditions

Because most counter workers are on duty less than thirty hours a week, some work only a few hours a day. Many work split breakfast-dinner shifts and have a few hours off in the middle of the day. This flexible schedule enables students to fit working hours around classes. Evening, weekend, and holiday work is often required.

Food counter workers must work quickly and effectively under pressure during busy periods. The ability to function as a member of a team, to stand for long periods of time, and to perform tasks within a restricted area is important in this job. Unlike food servers, food counter workers do not handle heavy trays, but are exposed to minor injuries from sharp implements or flatware, wet floors, hot utensils, or splashing of hot grease.

Training, Other Qualifications and Advancement

For counter jobs that require totaling bills and making change, employers prefer to hire people who are good in arithmetic and have attended high school, although a diploma usually is not necessary. Managers of fast food restaurants often hire high school students as part-time counter workers. Cafeterias have no specific educational requirements for counter jobs.

Most counter workers acquire their skills on the job by observing and working with more experienced workers. Some employers, including most fast-food restaurants, use self-study instructional booklets and audiovisual aids to train new employees.

A neat and pleasant personal appearance are important attributes for counter workers, because they deal with the public. Good health and physical stamina also are needed to stand most of the time and work at a fast pace during busy periods. State laws often require counter workers to obtain health certificates stating they are free of contagious diseases.

Opportunities for advancement are limited in small eating places. Some counter workers move into higher paying jobs and learn new skills by transferring to a larger restaurant. Advancement can be to a cashier, cook, food server, counter or fountain supervisor, or, for counter workers in cafeterias, to line supervisor. Many large companies, such as nationwide hamburger chains, operate formal management-training programs, while others offer informal on-the-job training. Dependable counter workers who show leadership abilities may qualify for these programs.

Employment Outlook

Job openings for food counter workers are expected to be plentiful in the coming years. Most openings will come from the need to replace workers who find jobs in other occupations, retire, or die. Because many counter workers are students who work part time and leave the occupation after graduation, turnover is high.

Employment in counter work is expected to increase faster than the average for all occupations through the year 2006, as population growth and rising personal incomes create more business for eating places. Also, with more women joining the work force, families may increasingly find dining out a welcome convenience. Expansion of the restaurant industry, particularly the fast-food segment, will create many job openings. Therefore, jobs should be relatively plentiful and easy to find.

Earnings

Full-time counter attendants and fast food workers had median weekly earnings (including any tips) of about $220 in 1996. The middle 50 percent earned between $190 and $270, while the highest 10 percent earned over $360 a week. Although some counter attendants receive part of their earnings as tips, fast food workers generally do not. Tips usually average between ten and twenty percent of patrons' checks. Counter workers often receive free meals at work and may be furnished with uniforms.

The principal union organizing food counter workers is the Hotel Employees and Restaurant Employees International Union (AFL-CIO).

CHAPTER 8

MIDDLE-LEVEL POSITIONS

Middle-level positions in the food service industry generally require some experience. On-the-job training is usually provided for the recently hired.

BARTENDERS

A bartender's career offers excellent opportunities to meet people while working in any one of many types of establishments. The duties of a bartender encompass both the preparation and service aspects of a food service operation.

Nature of the Work

A bartender must be a master of mixology. He or she is required to know and remember hundreds of beverage recipes to please people from all walks of life. Gold Cadillacs, Harvey Wallbangers, and Singapore Slings are merely a few of the exotic cocktails represented in the art of mixology, or bartending. By combining, in exact proportion, ingredients selected from a variety of liquors and mixes, bartenders can create these wild concoctions to please and delight their customers. A well-stocked bar contains many types and brands of liquor and soft drinks, fruit juices, cream, soda, and tonic water. Also, bartenders serve beer, wine, and a wide variety of nonalcoholic beverages.

Bartenders fill drink orders from food servers waiting on customers seated in the restaurant or lounge, in addition to serving patrons sitting at the bar.

Some people prefer their cocktails a certain way, so bartenders are often asked to mix drinks to suit a customer's particular taste. Most bartenders are required to know dozens of drink recipes and be capable of mixing drinks accurately by sight alone in order to serve drinks quickly, without wasting anything, even during the busiest periods. In addition to mixing and serving drinks, bartenders may be called upon to serve limited food items or snacks to customers seated at the bar, collect payment, operate the cash register, and clean up when customers leave.

Many large operations are now using equipment that mixes drinks automatically. However, bartenders still must be efficient and knowledgeable to handle unusual orders and to work when the automatic equipment is not functioning.

Bartenders are usually responsible for ordering and maintaining an inventory of liquor, mixes, and other bar supplies. They also arrange the bottles and glassware into attractive, geometric displays and wash glassware.

Bartenders employed in large restaurants or hotels may have bartender helpers to assist them with their many duties. Bartender helpers keep the bar supplied with liquor, mixes, and ice; stock refrigerators with beer and liquor; and replace empty beer kegs with full ones. Their duties also include keeping the area behind the bar clean and removing empty bottles and trash.

Bartenders are expected to ensure that the state and local laws concerning the serving of alcoholic beverages are strictly observed.

Because many bartenders own their own taverns or bars, they must keep their own business records and hire, train, and direct staff.

Working Conditions

Many bartenders work more than forty hours per week; and night work, weekend work, and split shifts are common. For many bartenders, however, the opportunity for friendly conversation with customers and the possibility of some day managing or owning a bar or restaurant of their own more than offsets these disadvantages. For others, the opportunity to get part-time employment is important.

Because bartenders play a significant role in making an establishment attractive to customers, a pleasant outgoing personality is a must for their career. In addition to understanding and liking all kinds of people, a bartender must have an excellent memory for faces, names, and recipes. Many bartenders pride themselves on being able to fill any drink order without looking up a recipe, and they are able to mix and serve drinks with a flair, a quality which helps make them popular with customers and employers alike.

A good bartender must be able to work accurately and rapidly, often mixing drinks by eye alone. Busy periods in popular operations can create considerable pressure, making a cool efficiency, coupled with attention to detail, an occupational necessity.

Some state and local regulations require that a bartender be at least twenty-one years of age, and many employers prefer job applicants to be twenty-five or older.

Because a bartender stands for hours, good physical condition is necessary. Better than average strength is sometimes needed to lift heavy cases of liquors or mixes.

Places of Employment

In 1996, 390,000 bartenders were employed in the United States. Most of these bartenders worked in restaurants and bars, others were employed in hotels and private clubs. Approximately ten percent were self-employed.

Several thousand people, many of whom also work in other occupations or attend college, tend bar part time. Often they serve at banquets and private parties, which are held at restaurants, hotels, or even private homes.

The majority of bartenders work in the urban population centers York, California, Illinois, and other large states, but many are employed in small communities. Seasonal employment is available in vacation resorts, and some bartenders migrate between summer and winter resorts rather than remain in one area the entire year.

Training, Other Qualifications, and Advancement

Most bartenders learn their trade on the job. Preparing drinks at home can be good practice, but it does not qualify a person to be a bartender. Besides knowing a variety of cocktail recipes, bartenders must know how to stock a bar properly and be familiar with state and local laws concerning the sale of alcoholic beverages.

People who wish to become bartenders can get valuable experience by working as bartender helpers, dining room attendants, or food servers. By observing a bartender at work, they can learn how to mix drinks and do most of the other bartending tasks.

Some schools offer short courses in bartending that include instruction on state and local laws and regulations, cocktail recipes, attire, conduct, and stocking a bar. Some of these schools even help their graduates find jobs.

Because they deal with the public, bartenders should have a pleasant personality and a neat and clean appearance. Physical stamina is necessary, because they stand while working and must lift heavy kegs of beer or cases of beverages.

Generally, bartenders must be at least twenty-one years of age, although some employers prefer those who are twenty-five or older. Some states demand health certificates ensuring bartenders are free from contagious diseases. In some instances, bartenders must be bonded. Most employers require bartenders to have a high school diploma.

Neighborhood bars, small restaurants, and resorts usually offer a beginner the best entry opportunities. After acquiring experience, a bartender may wish to work in a large restaurant or cocktail lounge, where salaries are higher and promotion opportunities are greater. Promotional opportunities in this field are limited; however, it is possible to advance to head bartender, wine steward, or beverage manager. Some bartenders open their own businesses.

Employment Outlook

Through the year 2006, employment of bartenders is expected to increase about as fast as the average for all occupations. In addition to job openings caused by employment growth, several thousand jobs will arise annually from the need to replace experienced bartenders who retire, die, or leave the occupation for other reasons. Because many bartenders are students or others who don't plan a career in this occupation, job turnover is relatively high.

The demand for bartenders will increase as new restaurants, hotels, and bars open in response to population growth and as spending on food and beverages outside the home increases commensurately.

Higher average incomes and more leisure time will allow people to go out for dinner or cocktails more often and to take more vacations. Also, with both spouses working, families are finding dining out a welcome convenience.

Earnings

Full-time bartenders had median weekly earnings (including tips) of about $310 in 1996. The middle 50 percent earned from

$230 and $400; the top 10 percent earned at least $520 a week. Also, bartenders employed in public bars may receive more than half of their earnings as tips.

Often bartenders receive free meals at work and may be furnished bar jackets or complete uniforms.

The principal union organizing and representing bartenders is the Hotel Employees and Restaurant Employees International Union (AFL-CIO).

Related Occupations

The duties of a bartender include taking orders, serving drinks, and collecting payment from customers. Other workers who serve customers include short-order cooks, restaurant and coffee shop managers, sales clerks, and food servers.

COOKS AND CHEFS

Cooks and chefs are the artists and administrators of the food service industry. Some of the most creative and interesting jobs of the entire industry belong to them. There is a strong demand for talented, well-trained cooks and chefs all over the country.

Nature of the Work

A reputation for serving fine food is an asset to any restaurant, whether it prides itself on home cooking or exotic foreign cuisine. Cooks and chefs are largely responsible for the reputation a restaurant acquires. Although the term *chef* and *cook* often are used interchangeably, the professional chef generally is a far more skilled, trained, and experienced person. Many chefs have earned fame for both themselves and the restaurants or hotels where they work because of their skill in creating new dishes and improving on the familiar ones.

The size and kind of restaurant will define the cook's duties. Smaller restaurants usually feature a limited number of easy-to-prepare, short-order specialities and ready-made desserts from a nearby bakery. Usually, one cook prepares all the food with the help of a short-order cook and one or two kitchen helpers. Here the cook, in addition to food preparation, may be responsible for purchasing, menu planning, and supervision of kitchen staff.

In large eating establishments, which usually have more varied menus and prepare more of the food they serve, the chef or executive chef is usually in charge of everybody and everything involved in the preparation process. The chef is responsible for techniques, supplies, and, to a great extent, profits. Supervisory responsibilities may include direction of several cooks, each one a specialist in the preparation of one part of a meal—soups, sauces, meats, vegetables, or pastries—and a large staff of helpers and assistants. In addition, the chef may be called upon to decide the size of servings, create menus, develop new recipes, and purchase all food supplies.

Working Conditions

Working conditions vary by organization and location. Many kitchens have modern equipment, convenient work areas, and air conditioning. But others, particularly older and smaller eating places, are frequently marginally equipped and poorly ventilated. Some safety hazards include cooking heat and sharp implements, but good safety standards have reduced accident risks in most organizations. Other variations in working conditions depend on the type and quantity of food being prepared and local laws governing food service operations. In the majority of kitchens, however, cooks stand most of the time, lift heavy pots and kettles, and work near hot ovens and ranges.

Cooks and chefs are often called upon to work holidays, late evenings, and weekends in restaurants. However, work hours in offices, factories, or other food service institutions might be more regular. Cooks employed in public and private schools usually work during the school year only, normally for nine to ten months.

Places of Employment

Approximately 3.4 million cooks and chefs were employed in 1996. The majority worked in restaurants and hotels. But jobs are available almost everywhere food is prepared for consumption outside the home, including schools, colleges, hospitals, nursing homes, sanitariums, department stores, and airports. Government agencies, factories, private clubs, steamships, and many other kinds of organizations also employ cooks and chefs.

Training, Other Qualifications, and Advancement

Most cooks work in an unskilled position, such as kitchen helper, and acquire their skills on the job. However, more and more cooks are obtaining their training through high school and post-high school vocational programs. Cooks also are trained in apprenticeship programs offered by professional associations and trade unions. A three-year apprenticeship program is administered by local offices of the American Culinary Federation in cooperation with local employers and junior colleges or vocational-education institutions. Also, some large hotels and restaurants operate their own training programs for new employees.

Although little experience is necessary to become an assistant or fry cook, many years of training and experience are necessary to achieve the level of skill required of an executive chef in a fine restaurant. Even though a high school diploma is not *required* for beginning jobs, it is recommended for those planning a career as a cook or chef. High school or vocational school courses in business arithmetic and business administration are particularly helpful. To acquire experience, high school students can work part time in fast food or other restaurants.

People who have taken courses in commercial food preparation will find this an advantage when seeking jobs in large restaurants and hotels where the hiring standards are high.

Some high school vocational programs offer this training. Courses also are given by trade schools, vocational centers, junior colleges, universities, professional associations, hotel-management groups, and trade unions. Some programs present a training period of only a few months. Others may require two or more years of study. In some cases, courses are open only to high school graduates.

The armed forces also are a good source of training, and they present an excellent opportunity to acquire experience in food service work.

Although curricula may vary, students usually spend most of their time learning to prepare food through actual practice. Training programs often include courses in selection and storage of food, use of leftovers, determination of portion size, menu planning, food cost control, and purchasing food supplies in quantity. In addition, students learn hotel and restaurant sanitation and public health rules for handling food. Training in supervisory and management skills sometimes is emphasized in courses offered by private vocational schools, professional associations, and in university programs.

In cooperation with school service divisions of state departments of education, many school districts provide on-the-job training and sometimes summer workshops for cafeteria workers who wish to become cooks. Some junior colleges, state departments of education, and school associations also offer training programs. Cafeteria employees who have participated in these training programs often are selected for jobs as cooks.

People who want to become chefs or cooks should be able to work as a member of a team and withstand the pressure and strain of working in close quarters during busy periods. A keen sense of taste and smell, the physical stamina to stand for hours at a time, and personal cleanliness also are important characteristics. Most states demand health certificates indicating that cooks and chefs are free from any contagious diseases.

Advancement opportunities for cooks are better than for most other food service occupations. Many cooks acquire high paying positions and new cooking skills by moving from one operation to another. Others gradually advance to chef positions or supervisory or management positions, particularly in hotels, clubs, or the larger, more elegant restaurants. Some eventually enter business as caterers or restaurant owners; others may become instructors in vocational programs in high schools, junior and community colleges, and other academic institutions.

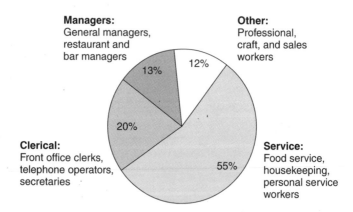

To provide the services guests expect, hotels and motels employ large numbers of clerks, managers and service workers.

Source: United States Department of Labor, Bureau of Labor Statistics

Employment Outlook

Employment of cooks and chefs is expected to increase faster than the average for all occupations through the year 2006. In addition to employment growth, thousands of job openings arise annually from the need to replace experienced workers who retire, die, or transfer to other occupations. Small restaurants, school cafeterias, and other eating places with simple food preparation requirements will provide the greatest number of starting jobs for cooks.

The demand for cooks and chefs will increase as the population grows and people eat out more often. More leisure time and higher personal incomes will allow people to go out for meals more often and to take more vacations. Dining out is becoming a more welcome convenience as more women join the work force.

Earnings

In 1996, hourly wage rates ranged from $10.00 to $12.00 for chefs, from $6.00 to $8.00 for cooks of various types, and from $5.50 to $7.00 for assistant cooks, according to a survey conducted by the National Restaurant Association.

Pay rates of chefs and cooks vary depending on the part of the country and the type of establishment in which they work. Wages are generally higher in the West and in large well-known restaurants and hotels. Cooks and chefs in famous restaurants earn much more than the minimum rates, and several chefs with national reputations earn more than $40,000 a year.

The principal union organizing and representing cooks and chefs is the Hotel Employees and Restaurant Employees Interactional Union (AFL-CIO).

Related Occupations

Cooks and chefs are not the only workers who create and then display a product to its best advantage. Other workers similarly involved include artists, clothes designers, and decorators. In addition, cooks and chefs may manage facilities ranging in size from a two-person sandwich shop to a large restaurant's kitchen employing dozens of people. Other workers with similar management responsibilities include food service directors, executive housekeepers, and pursers.

MEATCUTTERS

Meatcutters prepare meat, fish, and poultry in supermarkets or wholesale food outlets. When the animal carcasses are shipped from a meatpacking plant or central distribution center, they are cut into quarters to facilitate handling. Meatcutters then divide the quarters into primal cuts, such as rounds, loins, and ribs, with a band saw. They use knives and saws to separate these large cuts into serving-size portions, such as steaks, roasts, and chops. Boneless cuts are divided by knives, slicers, or power cutters while band saws are used on bony pieces. Meat trimmings are ground into hamburger. Meatcutters also may prepare sausage and coined beef. Meatcutters in retail food stores may be required to stock meat-display cases and assist customers.

Working Conditions

Meatcutters work in cold rooms designed to prevent meat from spoiling. The low temperatures and the need to stand for long periods of time and to lift heavy pieces of meat demand physical strength and stamina. Meatcutters must be careful when working with sharp tools, especially those that are powered.

Health and safety standards require clean and sanitary work areas.

Places of Employment

In 1996, approximately 369,000 people worked as meatcutters. Most are employed in retail food stores. The rest work in wholesale stores, restaurants, hotels, hospitals, and other institutions. Jobs are located in almost every city and town in the nation.

Training, Other Qualifications, and Advancement

Most meatcutters acquire their skills on the job. Although many are informally trained, most learn through apprenticeship programs. A few meatcutters learn their skills by attending private schools specializing in this trade. However, graduates of these schools often need additional training and experience to work as meatcutters.

Generally, on-the-job trainees begin by doing odd jobs, such as removing bones and fat from retail cuts. Under the guidance of skilled meatcutters, they learn about the proper use of tools and equipment and how to prepare various cuts. After demonstrating skill with tools, they learn to divide quarters into primal cuts and to divide primal cuts into retail and individual portions. Trainees may learn how to cut and prepare fish and poultry, roll and tie roasts, prepare sausage, and cure meat. Later, they may learn marketing operations such as inventory control, meat buying, and recordkeeping.

Meatcutters who learn the trade through apprenticeship programs generally complete two years of supervised on-the-job training that may be supplemented by classroom work. When the training period ends, apprentices are given a meatcutting test, which is observed by their employer. In union shops, a union member also is present during the exam. Apprentices who pass the text qualify as meatcutters. Those who fail the exam may repeat it at a later time. In some areas, apprentices may become meatcutters without completing the entire training program, if they can pass the meatcutting test.

Most employers prefer applicants who have a high school diploma and the potential to develop into meat department managers. Other skills important in meatcutting are manual dexterity, good depth perception, color discrimination, and good eye-hand coordination. A pleasant personality, a neat appearance, and the ability to communicate clearly are important qualifications when meatcutters wait on customers. Better-than-average strength is needed to lift heavy pieces of meat. A health certificate indicating that the applicant is free of contagious diseases may be required for employment.

Meatcutters may progress to supervisory jobs, such as meat department managers in supermarkets. A few become meat buyers for wholesalers and supermarket chains. Some cutters become grocery store managers or open their own meat markets.

Employment Outlook

The number of meatcutters is expected to grow more slowly than the average for all occupations through the year 2006. Nevertheless, thousands of entry jobs will be available as experienced workers retire, die, or leave the occupation for other reasons.

Employment of meatcutters in food stores will be limited by central cutting—the practice of cutting and wrapping meat for several stores at one location. Central cutting, which permits meatcutters to specialize in both a type of meat and a type of cut, increases efficiency. More central cutting also is expected to be done in meatpacking plants, thus reducing the amount of meat cut, and the need for meatcutters, in food stores.

Earnings

In 1996, meatcutters had median weekly earnings of $370. The middle 50 percent earned between $280 and $520 a week. The highest paid 10 percent earned more than $740 a week.

Meatcutters employed by retail grocery stores are generally among the higher-paid workers in this occupation.

Many cutters are members of the United Food and Commercial Workers International Union.

Related Occupations

Meatcutters must be able to do both skilled hand and machine work and have some knowledge of processes and techniques involved in preparing food. Other occupations in food preparation that require similar skills are bakers, cooks, butchers of chicken and fish, and kitchen supervisors.

CHAPTER 9

MANAGEMENT POSITIONS

Experience and education are two attributes that are usually required for qualification for higher-level management positions in the food service industry.

RESTAURANT MANAGER

The success of food service operations depends largely on the skills, abilities, and imagination of their management. Restaurant management can be demanding, varied, fast-paced, and highly rewarding.

A modern restaurant is a complex operation with the restaurant manager at its hub. Restaurant managers must be able to work efficiently behind the scenes, coordinating a wide variety of staff and administrative functions. They must be able to work effectively with the public as spokespeople, promoters, and goodwill ambassadors.

Restaurant managers are responsible for hiring, training and directing restaurant staff members; determining work schedules; and setting personnel policies. In addition, they may be responsible for administering employee benefit programs. Keeping abreast of costs and maintaining accurate inventories are essential because managers are responsible for the purchase of all supplies and equipment.

A restaurant manager must have good business skills and know how to set prices to make a profit. He or she must take responsibility for the restaurant's accounts and records, and must know and comply with all food service laws and regulations, especially those concerned with licensing, health, and sanitation. A manager must know every aspect of the restaurant business thoroughly because it is the manager who is called on to act as troubleshooter for all restaurant operations.

Supervising advertising programs and working with the food production staff to create menus with customer appeal are part of the restaurant manager's duty. The manager must stay in touch with changing needs and wants in the marketplace, help establish the "personality" of the restaurant, and be adept in dealing with the public, listening to suggestions, and handling complaints with diplomacy.

In a large restaurant, many of the duties listed above would be taken care of by the assistant manager, food production manager, personnel director, menu planner, merchandising supervisor, or director of recipe development. The smaller the operation, the more diversified the duties of a restaurant manager.

Working Conditions

Night and weekend work are very common to a restaurant manager who may work anywhere from forty to ninety or more hours a week. Restaurant managers sometimes experience the pressures of coordinating a wide range of functions. However, the working environment is usually clean, well-lighted, and air conditioned.

Training, Other Qualifications, and Advancement

Experience generally is the most important consideration in selecting managers. However, employers are increasingly emphasizing college education. Completion of a two-year associate degree program at a junior or community college, or a bachelor's degree program in hotel and restaurant management at a four-year college or university, will enable applicants to enter restaurant management at a higher level. In 1996, more than 160 colleges and universities offered four-year programs in this field. Because more aspiring managers are seeking formal training, applicants to these programs may face increasing competition in the coming years. Many junior colleges, technical institutes, and the Educational Institute of the American Hotel and Motel Association also have courses in management work that provide a person with a good background.

Included in many college programs in hotel and restaurant management are courses in hotel administration, accounting, economics, data processing, housekeeping, food service management, catering, and hotel maintenance engineering. Part-time or summer work in hotels and restaurants is encouraged. The experience gained and the contact with employers may benefit students when they seek a job after graduation.

Managers should have initiative, self-discipline, and the ability to organize and direct the work of others. They must be able to solve problems and concentrate on details.

Sometimes, large restaurant chains sponsor specialized, on-the-job management-training programs that enable trainees to rotate among various departments and receive a thorough knowledge of the restaurant's operation.

Restaurant chains may offer better opportunities for advancement than independently owned establishments, because employees can transfer to another hotel or motel in the chain or to the central office if an opening occurs.

Employment Outlook

Food service managers held approximately 493,000 jobs in 1996. Employment of restaurant managers is expected to grow faster than the average for all occupations through the year 2006 as additional restaurants are built and chain and franchise operations spread. However, most openings will occur as experienced managers die, retire, or leave the occupation. Seasonal employment opportunities will be available in resort establishments that are open only part of the year.

Applicants with college degrees in hotel and restaurant administration will have an advantage in seeking entry-level positions and, later, advancement.

Earnings

Based on a survey conducted for the National Restaurant Association, the median base salary of restaurant managers was $30,000 a year in 1995, but managers of the largest restaurants and institutional food service facilities often had annual salaries in excess of $50,000.

Managers of fast food restaurants had a median base salary of $23,000 a year. Managers of full-menu restaurants with table service earned a median base salary of $27,000, and managers of commercial and institutional cafeterias earned $26,000 a year in 1995.

In addition to a salary, most managers received an annual bonus or incentive payment based on their performance. In 1995, most of these payments ranged between $2,000 and $10,000 a year.

The median base salary of assistant managers was $23,000 a year in 1995, but ranged from $21,000 in fast food restaurants to more than $27,000 in some of the largest restaurants and food service facilities. Annual bonus or incentive payments of most assistant managers ranged between $1,000 and $4,000 a year.

Manager trainees had a median base salary of $21,000 a year in 1995, but they had salaries of more than $30,000 in some of the largest restaurants and food service facilities. Annual bonus or incentive payments of most trainees averaged $900.

Most salaried restaurant and food service managers received free meals, sick leave, health and life insurance, and one weeks of paid vacation a year, depending on length of service.

DIETITIANS

Dietitians provide nutritional counseling to individuals and groups. They set up and supervise food service systems for institutions such as hospitals and schools. They promote sound eating habits through education and research.

Among dietitians, major areas of specialization include administration, education, research, and clinical and community dietetics.

Administrative dietitians are the ones the food service industry is interested in. They apply the principles of nutrition and sound management to large-scale meal planning and preparation, such as that done in hospitals, prisons, company cafeterias, schools, and other institutions. They supervise the planning, preparation, and service of meals. They select, train, and direct food service supervisors and workers. They also budget for and purchase food, equipment, and supplies; enforce sanitary and safety regulations; and prepare records and reports.

Working Conditions

Dietitians in commercial food service have somewhat irregular hours. Dietitians spend much of their time in clean, well-lighted, and well-ventilated areas such as research laboratories, classrooms, or offices near food preparation areas.

Employment

About 58,000 persons worked as dietitians in 1996. Part-time work is available in this field. About fifteen percent of all dietitians work part time.

Heath care facilities, including hospitals, nursing homes, and clinics, are major employers of dietitians, accounting for just over half of all jobs in 1996.

Training, Other Qualifications, and Advancement

The basic educational requirements for dietitians is a bachelor's degree, with a major in foods and nutrition or institutional management. Required college courses include food and nutrition, institutional management, chemistry, microbiology, physiology, sociology, and economics. It also is possible to prepare for this profession by receiving an advanced degree in nutrition, food service management, or related sciences and providing evidence of qualifying work experience.

Job Outlook

Employment of dietitians is expected to grow faster than the all occupations through the year 2006 to meet the rapidly expanding needs of hospitals, long-term care facilities, and food service operations.

According to the American Dietetic Association, median annual income for registered dietitians in 1995 varied in practice area as follows: clinical nutrition, $34,131; food and nutrition management, $42,964; community nutrition, $33,902; consultation and business, $43,374; and education and research, $42,784. Salaries also vary by years in practice, educational level, geographic region, and size of community.

Dietitians usually receive benefits such as paid vacations, sick leave, holidays, health insurance, and retirement benefits.

CHAPTER 10

RUNNING YOUR OWN BUSINESS

OPENING A RESTAURANT

Operating a restaurant is not an easy thing to do. Almost every week, two hundred new restaurants open in the United States. One year later, only forty will still be in business. A twenty percent success rate is not an encouraging figure, but this does not seem to discourage would-be restaurateurs. The benefits and satisfactions of a successful operation apparently are a very powerful lure.

Although no one can offer sure secrets to success, there are steps one can take to avoid common pitfalls and help ensure a successful venture.

DEVELOPING A PLAN

A plan of action is the most important step in opening a restaurant. A workable restaurant plan that outlines a concept in food service as well as a marketing research effort will be a critical aid to even the most experienced food service professionals. This well-thought-out plan will help: calculate precise initial investment requirements; apply for financing; project operating expenses; and project break-even sales figures.

The first part of the plan should address the following questions:

- What kind of food will be served?
- What is the general price range?
- What type of service (fast-food, self-service, cafeteria, counter, table service) will be offered?
- What menu items will be offered?
- What kind of atmosphere is desired?
- Who are the anticipated clientele?
- What cooking methods will be used?
- What size staff is necessary?
- What kind of inventory is required?
- What hours will the restaurant operate?
- What are the projected sales?
- What amount of food should be prepared on site?

Because the new owner must find property that will adhere to the proposed layout and operation, it is necessary to consider the above questions before a specific site is chosen.

DEVELOPING A MARKETING STUDY

Prospective restaurant owners often have a concept in mind, but fail to do adequate marketing research to determine whether their ideas match the needs of the neighborhood.

That's what marketing research is—a study of consumer preferences. Marketing research also is an assessment of the local business environment. A market investigation will help the prospective restaurant owner ascertain if a real demand exists for a particular kind of restaurant. It also will tell if there is so much demand that an oversupply of similar establishments will mean fierce competition.

Once you know who the potential customers are; what percentage of the population they represent; the competition you are up against; and also the business traffic patterns by hours of the day, days of the week, and a weekday versus a weekend schedule; you will be in a better position to supply the needs to your customers and to compete with other restaurants in the locality.

Most of this information can be self-compiled. The U.S. Census of Population gives demographic profiles, income levels, and housing patterns for the nation as a whole and by segments—down to city blocks. The data are reasonably priced and available in printed form or by computer. For a small additional fee, the U.S. Bureau of the Census will prepare an individualized computer printout. The Bureau has offices throughout the United States and holds numerous workshops and conferences on how to use the data.

The Conference Board in New York City annually publishes a *Census of Selected Service Industries.* This publication states the number of establishments in an area, their total receipts, and payrolls. Your local chamber of commerce and the National Restaurant Association Information Service and Library (Washington, D.C.) have additional data, ranging from reports and surveys on financial considerations to kitchen design.

Doing such a market survey takes time. But it's time well spent. The survey can provide prospective owners with two extremely important functions:

1. It can keep you from opening a restaurant in a location where success is impossible.
2. It can greatly aid your case when you seek help in funding from financial institutions.

CHOOSING A SITE

Once a market is chosen and a suitable concept decided on, the prospective restaurateur should concentrate on selecting a specific site. A restaurant's success probably depends most on a proper location. This location should position the restaurant where it can best attract and serve its anticipated clientele.

As you consider locations, ask yourself:

- Is the space visible from the street?
- Are parking arrangements available?
- What type of business is expected?
- Are there hidden costs involved in remodeling or construction?
- What type of businesses are nearby (are they good generators of potential customers)?
- Is public transportation available (do taxi cabs frequent the area)?
- What are the peak hours of traffic?
- Are there plans for growth in the area?
- What are the average sales of competitors in the area?
- How many households are in the area?

Scrutinize your location site thoroughly. Obtain every possible means of helpful data from:

- the Department of Commerce
- the Small Business Association
- real estate agencies
- your restaurant consultant
- your accountant
- your banker
- your insurance agent

Many prospective restaurant owners believe that they can more easily enter the food service industry by buying a restaurant that is already in operation. Considerable expense can be saved by buying a building that doesn't need extensive remodeling. That eliminates the high cost of complying with local building codes.

Current owners, who are running good operations but can't make their interest payment, may provide an excellent opportunity for a prospective restaurant owner. As little as ten to thirty percent of the original construction costs may be all it takes to purchase a bankrupt restaurant. The new owner probably will be able to realize good profits because there will be less debt to service.

However, a potential buyer should double check the reasons given for selling the business, no matter how attractive it seems. The seller may offer poor health or retirement as the reason for selling, but through careful study of local conditions, the prospective buyer might discover the real reason to be:

- declining business
- lack of competitive strength
- changes in the neighborhood
- obsolete products or facilities
- highway construction or rerouting
- inability to collect accounts receivable
- problems with creditors
- expiring lease or franchise

CODES, ORDINANCES, AND PERMITS

During the site-selection process, information about local codes, ordinances, permits, and licenses should be obtained. A fire clearance, for example, depends on inspection. Some common codes include: fire, health, parking, occupancy, garbage, sewage, and loading zone.

Both health and building codes usually require cost estimates and blueprints to be submitted before construction. If these are well-prepared and planned, costly after-construction alterations will be minimized.

Several licenses also will be necessary before opening a new restaurant:

- A fictitious name license, or DBA (Doing Business as... form will probably be needed if you plan to operate under a name other than your own.
- A business license or a sales tax license is required by some states.
- A liquor or beer and wine license is necessary if you plan to serve alcoholic beverages. These licenses usually require fingerprinting, an inspection, and often a period of time for local citizens to file any objections to the license. Some jurisdictions demand that you buy a license from a former owner rather than apply for a new one. Registration with the Internal Revenue Service through form 11 is compulsory for this license.

MENU PLANNING

The menu performs a major function for every restaurant. The many purposes of a menu include:

- defining your restaurant
- reflecting your concept
- attracting your customers
- providing a guide for ordering, purchasing, and estimating income
- determining the layout of the kitchen
- determining how skilled a staff is necessary
- determining the level of service necessary
- determining storage requirements
- determining special equipment needed

- setting the tone of your restaurant and helping to furnish and decorate it appropriately

The menu should never be static. It should be influenced by the following considerations:

- potential clientele
- seasonal availability
- community preferences
- suitable combinations of dishes
- alternatives for leftovers

Those restaurateurs who can limit the menu and still do a high-volume business will reap the greatest profits, but restaurant image and appeal sometimes prohibit this.

Price is also an important factor when drawing up your menu. Overpricing has killed many new operations. A general rule often used in the food service industry is that a menu price should not be more than double or triple the wholesale food cost.

Records on how frequently menu items are served help owners reorder the correct quantity of food. Many restaurateurs say personal computer systems often pay for themselves by tracking menu items.

THE KITCHEN PLAN AND ITS EQUIPMENT

The kitchen is vitally important to any food service operation, and careful planning should be given to it.

The kitchen plan should include:

- work space for food preparation
- adequate space to pass food from the cooks to the food servers
- sufficient aisle space for food servers to deliver the food to the patrons

- cleanup center for washing dishes and disposing of garbage
- separate area for delivery of inventory

Costs for new kitchen equipment can run into thousands of dollars. Here are some commonly purchased items:

- short order griddles or grills
- broilers
- rapid cooking conventional ovens
- double-decker ovens
- ranges
- dryers
- microwave ovens
- full-size refrigerators
- walk-in freezers (7 × 10 foot)
- dishwashers

Equipment companies usually do not extend more than sixty to ninety days credit to customers, so many of these purchases must come from start-up capital. Sometimes equipment leasing arrangements are possible. These allow you to stretch payments over a longer period but usually include substantial interest charges.

Remember that price is not the only consideration when choosing equipment. Other important factors that should be weighed include:

- manufacturer's reliability
- repair service availability
- quality of repair

GETTING A GOOD FINANCIAL START

It takes a lot of money to open a restaurant, and there is no guarantee of success. Eighty-five percent of investment costs go to opening expenses, which include:

- wiring
- plumbing
- painting
- labor
- materials
- kitchen fixtures and equipment
- furniture
- two months lease deposit

Whether you decide on equity financing, which is money from investors, or debt financing, which is money from a financial establishment, obtaining it is difficult. Most restaurateurs look to both sources for financing.

A typical bank loan requires furnishing a great deal of information including:

- a detailed report on the loan's purpose
- personal financial statements
- a list of partners or corporate officers
- projected financial statements for the first one or two years

Most banks require you to find half the financing yourself. This can come from relatives, friends, business associates, or partners, but not from another loan. By demonstrating your viability with market studies and by having bookkeeping, accounting, and marketing systems in place, you may strengthen your position with a financial establishment.

The federal government is another source of potential financing. Although the process is often difficult, the loans can be below market interest rates and with longer payback periods. The Small Business Administration (SBA) will guarantee up to ninety percent of a commercial loan. On rare occasions, the SBA may make a direct loan if the applicant can prove he or she cannot find funding elsewhere.

No matter where you go for financing, it is a good idea to have enough capital to cover at least two to six months of payroll and food costs. One of the major causes of small business failures is insufficient financing.

When drawing up your financial requirements, make sure to include money for these common start-up costs:

- initial lease deposit or down payment on property
- remodeling or making improvements
- purchase of equipment and furnishings
- license payments
- utility and insurance deposits
- initial food inventory
- initial advertising
- consultant fees (lawyer, accountant, kitchen designer, menu designer, etc.)
- initial payroll and payroll taxes

Also, be sure to build a cushion for the unexpected, such as a delay in opening.

STAFFING

Many times potential restaurant owners overestimate their capabilities. Although sometimes it is necessary, it is difficult for an owner to be a personnel manager, financier, chef, food purchaser, tax expert, and public relations expert all at the same time. Interviewing, hiring, and training people can be a time-consuming and nerve-racking process, but time invested in this process at the beginning will pay off substantially in the end.

FRANCHISE OPPORTUNITIES

Many first-time restaurateurs are attracted by the opportunities of a restaurant franchise. The eighty percent survival rate of establishments franchised by reputable chains has a lot to do with their appeal. Franchised businesses account for billions in annual sales and nearly a third of total United States retail sales.

What Exactly Is a Restaurant Franchise?

Franchising is a form of licensing by which the owner (the franchisor) obtains distribution through affiliated dealers (the franchisees). Franchise agreements call for the parent company to give an independent businessperson rights to a successful restaurant concept and trademark, plus assistance in organizing, training, merchandising, and managing. In return for these rights and assistance, the franchisee pays the company a franchise fee and monthly royalties.

In recent years, it has become increasingly difficult to break into the franchise business, but it is not impossible.

Examine the Franchisor Carefully

The prospective restaurateur should examine the franchisor's claims and credentials as thoroughly as possible. Careful investigation into the backgrounds and current business practices of operations is essential. Comparison shopping should be done on many franchise packages to see where the best deals on franchise fees and royalties are offered.

A disclosure statement, sometimes called an offering circular or prospectus, is available from every franchisor. This disclosure statement will prove an invaluable help in comparing one franchise with another, understanding the risks involved, and learning what to expect and what not to expect from the franchise you finally decide on.

What to Look for in a Franchise Company

A reputable franchise company should provide:

- a site, usually a free-standing building that is leased to the franchisee
- exclusive territorial rights
- any exclusively developed equipment

- licensed use of trademark, inventory system, exclusive recipes, and techniques
- training courses and operations manuals
- continuing operations assistance for a specified percentage of gross sales
- inspections by company supervisors who will evaluate the operation
- consultation on reducing costs and improving efficiency and profits
- equipment
- suppliers
- advertising

Prospective franchisees are carefully interviewed by company sales directors who evaluate applicant's financial assets, character, and work history. Franchisors look for people who are eager to become independent operators, but who will conform to the company headquarter's guidelines. Applicants who meet these qualifications can expect to pay:

- an initial franchise fee
- continuing royalty fees, which can range from 2.5 to 8 percent of the unit gross sales
- advertising contributions of about 2 to 4 percent of gross sales
- food, labor, and paper costs
- equipment purchase or rental costs
- rent

The Value of an Attorney

Anyone considering entering into a franchise agreement should employ an attorney to determine if the contract's provisions protect his or her interests. Be certain the lawyer does a thorough job of checking out:

- the length of contract
- the royalty charges
- the fixed charges
- the purchasing requirements
- the quotas
- the arbitration privileges
- how the contract can be terminated
- how the company can terminate the franchisee

Franchising is an excellent way for a person without special skills to be trained in every aspect of the food service industry, but be certain that all the facts are checked thoroughly. The cost of legal advice at the outset is invariably less than the cost of later representation to solve legal problems that could have been avoided in the beginning.

CHAPTER 11

RELATED OCCUPATIONS
IN FOOD SERVICE

Aside from the obvious career positions in the food service industry like bartender, food server, and restaurant manager, there are positions available in this industry for a variety of skilled people. There is a growing industry need for the following: lawyers, accountants, public relations specialists, marketing managers, computer specialists, purchasing agents, quality assurance officers, and secretaries.

LAWYERS

Laws affect every aspect of our society, and this includes the food service industry. Lawyers should always be consulted before purchasing, opening, and selling a restaurant. As the food industry grows, the work of lawyers or attorneys takes on broader significance—they are employed to interpret the laws, rulings and regulations pertaining to the food service industry.

Many restaurants employ a lawyer full time. Known as a house counsel, this lawyer usually advises the company about legal questions that arise from business activities.

ACCOUNTANTS

Restaurant managers must have up-to-date financial information to make important decisions. Accountants and auditors prepare and analyze financial reports that furnish this kind of information. Accountants employed by large restaurant firms may travel extensively to audit or work for clients or branches of the firm. Employment is expected to grow faster than the average for these occupations through the year 2005 due to pressures of businesses to improve budgeting and accounting procedures.

PUBLIC RELATIONS SPECIALISTS

Public relations workers help food service businesses build and maintain a positive public reputation, which is crucial to the success of any food service operation. Public relations workers put together information that keeps the public aware of their organization's policies, activities, and accomplishments, and keeps managements aware of public attitudes. After preparing the information, they then contact people in the media who might be interested in printing, televising, or broadcasting their material. Preparing and delivering speeches, attending meetings and community activities, and traveling out of town will all be part of the job assigned to the public relations worker.

Creativity, initiative, and the ability to express thoughts clearly and simply are important traits of the public relations specialist. People who choose public relations as a career need an outgoing personality, self-confidence, and an understanding of human psychology.

MARKETING MANAGERS

Marketing managers are responsible for compiling information on the age, sex, and income level of a restaurant's potential clientele, as well as their dining habits and preferences. On this information, they base their decisions of whether a restaurant would do well in a certain area. Marketing managers consider customer preferences in order to suggest appropriate sales advertising techniques.

COMPUTER SPECIALISTS

Computer specialists play an increasingly important role in restaurants today. Inventory control, restaurant accounting, employee statistics, accounting, programming and advertising lists are all areas in which computers are being used more and more in the industry.

PURCHASING AGENTS

Purchasing agents are responsible for obtaining goods and services of the quality required at the lowest possible cost. Also, it is their job to see that adequate materials and supplies are always available.

Purchasing agents choose suppliers by comparing listings in catalogs, directories, and trade journals. They must meet with salespeople to discuss items to be purchased, examine samples, and attend demonstrations of equipment.

Purchasing agents must be able to analyze the technical data in suppliers' proposals to make buying decisions and spend large amounts of money responsibly. The job requires the ability to work independently and to work well with people. Purchasing agents need a good memory for details.

QUALITY ASSURANCE OFFICERS

In the food service industry, a quality assurance officer has a very important job. The cleanliness and sanitation practices of a food service operation are crucial elements to its success. The quality assurance officers are responsible for developing and implementing sanitation practices that will keep the restaurant in business.

ADMINISTRATIVE ASSISTANTS AND SECRETARIES

In large food service operations, administrative assistants and secretaries play a very important role. They perform a variety administrative and clerical duties so that their employers are free to work on other matters.

In addition to a solid grounding in secretarial skills, employers look for a good command of the English language and an aptitude for numbers. Because secretaries must be tactful in their dealings with many different people, discretion, judgment, organizational ability, and initiative are important attributes for the more responsible secretarial positions.

CHAPTER 12

OBTAINING A FOOD SERVICE POSITION

PLANNING YOUR CAREER

There is currently an abundance of job opportunities in the food service industry. This chapter will deal with the question of how to secure the right position for you. Here is a list of twelve steps you should follow to obtain a food service position:

1. Determine what kind of position you desire and are fitted for and what you would be most happy doing.
2. Plan an active campaign for securing that job.
3. Prepare a professionally typeset resume.
4. Inform business associates, your high school or college placement office, purveyors, private employment agencies, and friends that you are seeking employment in this field.
5. Secure all the information you can about companies that you are interested in by talking with people and conducting research.
6. Write a letter to each company and enclose a resume for consideration, or place telephone calls inquiring about employment opportunities.
7. Arrange for an interview.

8. Prepare for that interview, both in mental attitude and by physical appearance.
9. Go to the interview, and find out about the job.
10. Appraise yourself after the interview. Evaluate your answers to their questions, analyze your performance, and correct any negative statements that you made so you can do better in future interviews.
11. Write a thank you letter to the interviewer for the time and consideration given you.
12. Wait to hear from the company on the specified date; if you don't hear by then, contact the company.

THE RESUME

The purpose of a resume is to organize the relevant facts about yourself in a written presentation. Therefore, the resume should contain brief but sufficient information to inform a prospective employer of the following:

- what you are capable of
- What you have accomplished
- What knowledge you have
- what kind of position you are applying for (which can be specified in the resume or in a cover letter)

By providing this information, your resume will accomplish several objectives:

1. It will serve as an introduction.
2. It will save time for both applicant and interviewer.
3. It will serve as a focus for and improve your personal interview. When your assets are organized on paper, it will be easier to discuss them with assurance. Also, fumbling for dates and significant facts will be eliminated.

4. Having all the facts at your fingertips will help you avoid overstatements or understatements.
5. It will provide the interviewer with a visual reminder of what you covered verbally during the interview.

INTERVIEWING

The difference between a successful and unsuccessful job interview in the food service industry may depend on these seven crucial tips:

- Be on time for your interview.
- First impressions are very important. Treat the receptionist as well as your interviewer politely and respectfully.
- Dress appropriately for the interview. Personal grooming and cleanliness are a must for any food service position.
- A complete application is an important part of the interview process. Be sure to answer every question thoroughly and neatly.
- If you possess any special skills or talents, include them on the application. There may be a special position just for you.
- Show interest in the company, sit up straight, and maintain eye contact. One-word responses to questions, gum chewing, and smoking should be avoided.
- Don't be reluctant to ask questions. It's a sign of interest and enthusiasm.

Questions Often Asked by Food Service Employers During Interviews

Here are twenty questions that you should think about as part of your interview preparation.

1. What are your long-range career objectives? What do you see yourself doing five years from now?

2. What are the most important rewards you expect in your food service career?
3. Why did you choose the career for which you are preparing?
4. What is more important to you, the money or the type of job?
5. In your estimation, what are your greatest strengths and weaknesses?
6. How would you describe yourself? How would a friend? A professor?
7. What motivates you to put forth your greatest effort?
8. How has your past experience prepared you for your career?
9. Why should someone hire you?
10. What personal qualifications make you think you will be successful in your career?
11. How do you evaluate or determine success?
12. How can you contribute to our company?
13. What should be the relationship between a supervisor and those reporting to him or her?
14. Name two or three accomplishments that have given you the most satisfaction? Why?
15. What school subject did you like best and least? Why?
16. Do you have plans for continued study?
17. What is your most comfortable work environment?
18. Why did you choose to seek a position with this particular company?
19. What do you know about this company?
20. Do you have a geographical preference? Why?

FINDING OUT ABOUT POSITIONS IN FOOD SERVICE

Word-of-mouth is a great way to hear about a food service position. But it is far from the only way. Here is a list of job sources:

- professional associations (see also Appendix A)
- classified ads in newspapers, professional journals, and trade magazines (see also Appendix C)
- private employment agencies and recruiters (see also Appendix B)
- state employment services
- computer websites
- interviewers
- yellow pages of the telephone directory, industrial directories, and chamber of commerce lists
- U.S. Civil Service Commission
- unions
- local television and radio station announcements

Networking also can help you locate a job. Networking simply means to form a network of your friends, former teachers, business acquaintances, and anyone else who could help you, to keep an eye open for the job that will mean something to you. Make a list of these people's names and phone numbers. Ask them to help you in your job search. Keep in touch regularly, and ask if they have come across any leads. People who know owners and managers of the kinds of places where you want to work are the most valuable. Don't hesitate to ask them to let you know of job openings, and to put in a word for you as an introduction. Be sure to thank all of these contacts, whether they are able to steer you to a job or not; their interest and knowledge of you as a learner and a worker can be very valuable to you in other, future job searches as well.

PROFESSIONAL ASSOCIATIONS

The following is a list of national and state associations to contact for further information on opportunities in food service careers.

Other sources of information include local employers, your individual state employment service, any of the schools listed in Appendices D and E, and industry trade periodicals in Appendix C.

NATIONAL

American Culinary Federation
10 San Bartola Drive
P.O. Box 3466
St. Augustine, FL 32085
(904) 824-4468

American Dietetic Association
216 W. Jackson Boulevard,
Suite 800
Chicago, IL 60606
(312) 899-0040

American Hotel and Motel
Association
1201 New York Avenue, N.W.,
Suite 600
Washington, DC 20005
(202) 289-3100

American Society for Healthcare
Food Service
Administrators
One N. Franklin, 31 N.
Chicago, IL 60606
(312) 422-3870

Council on Hotel, Restaurant, and
Institutional Education
1200 Seventeenth Street, N.W.
Washington, DC 20036
(202) 331-5900

Council of Hotel and Restaurant
Trainers
RR1 Box 180-B
Bryant, IN 47326
(908) 998-6984

Food Service Marketing Institute
339 Main Street
P.O. Box 1048
Lake Placid, NY 12946
(518) 523-2942

Food Service and Packaging
Institute
1550 Wilson Boulevard,
Suite 918
Arlington, VA 22209
(703) 527-7505

The Hospitality and Information
Service
Meridian House
1630 Crescent Place, N.W.
Washington, DC 20009
(202) 232-3002

International Food Service
Executive Association
1100 S. State Road 7,
Suite 103
Margate, FL 33068
(954) 977-0767

National Association of College
and University Food
Services
Michigan State University
1405 S. Harrison, Suite 305
East Lansing, MI 48824
(517) 332-2494

National Restaurant Association
1200 Seventeenth Street, N.W.
Washington, DC 20036
(202) 331-5900

Society for Foodservice
Management
304 W. Liberty Street,
Suite 201
Louisville, KY 40202
(502) 583-3783

Travel Industry Association
of America
1100 New York Avenue,
Suite 450
Washington, DC 20005
(202) 408-8422

STATE

Alabama Restaurant Association
P.O. Box 241413
Montgomery, AL 36124
(334) 244-1320

Arizona Restaurant Association
2701 N. 16th Street, Suite 221
Phoenix, AZ 85006
(602) 234-0701

Arkansas Hospitality Association
P.O. Box 3866
603 Pulaski Street
Little Rock, AR 72203
(501) 376-2323

California Restaurant Association
3435 Wilshire Boulevard,
Suite 2230
Los Angeles, CA 90010
(213) 384-1200

Colorado Restaurant
Association
899 Logan Street #300
Denver, CO 80203
(303) 830-2972

Connecticut Restaurant
Association
731 Hebron Avenue
Glastonbury, CT 06033
(860) 633-8587

Delaware Restaurant Association
148 Glade Circle W.
Rehoboth Beach, DE 19714
(302) 227-7300

Restaurant Association of
Metropolitan Washington,
Inc.
7926 Jones Beach Drive,
Suite 530
McLean, VA 22102
(703) 356-1315

Florida Restaurant Association
230 S. Adams Street
Tallahassee, FL 32301
(850) 224-2250

Georgia Hospitality & Travel
Association
600 W. Peachtree Street,
Suite 1500
Atlanta, GA 30308
(404) 873-4482

Hawaii Restaurant Association
1188 Bishop Street,
Suite 1507
Honolulu, HI 96813
(808) 536-9105

Idaho Hospitality and Travel
Association
P.O. Box 7587
Boise, ID 83707
(208) 344-3465

Illinois Restaurant Association
200 N. LaSalle Street, Suite
880
Chicago, IL 60601
(312) 787-4000

Restaurant and Hospitality
Association of Indiana
115 W. Washington Street,
Suite 1165 S.
Indianapolis, IN 46204
(317) 673-4211

Iowa Hospitality
Association
606 Merle Hay Tower
Des Moines, IA 50310
(515) 276-1454

Kansas Restaurant and
Hospitalty Association
359 S. Hydraulic
Wichita, KS 67211
(316) 267-8383

Kentucky Restaurant
Association
512 Executive Park
Louisville, KY 40207
(502) 896-0464

Louisiana Restaurant
Association
2700 N. Arnoult Road
Metairie, LA 70002
(504) 454-2277

Maine Restaurant Association
P.O. Box 5060
5 Wade Street
Augusta, ME 04332
(207) 623-2178

Restaurant Association
of Maryland
7113 Ambassador Road
Baltimore, MD 21244
(410) 298-0011

Massachusetts Restaurant
Association
95-A Turnpike Road
Westborough, MA 01581
(508) 366-4144

Michigan Retsaurant Association
221 N. Pine Street
Lansing, MI 48933
(517) 372-5656

Hospitality Minnesota
871 Jefferson Avenue
St. Paul, MN 55102
(612) 222-7401

Mississippi Restaurant
Association
4506 Office Park Drive
Jackson, MS 39236
(601) 982-4281

Missouri Restaurant Association
4049 Pennsylvania Avenue
Kansas City, MO 64111
(816) 753-5222

Montana Restaurant Association
1537 Avenue D, Suite 320
Billings, MT 59102
(402) 256-1005

Nebraska Restaurant Association
5625 'O' Street Building,
Suite #7
Lincoln, NE 68510
(402) 483-2630

Nevada Restaurant Association
4820 Alpine Road,
Suite F-203
Las Vegas, NV 89107
(702) 878-2313

New Hampshire Lodging and
Restaurant Association
P.O. Box 1175
Concord, NH 03302
(603) 228-9585

New Jersey Restaurant
Association
One Executive Drive,
Suite 100
Somerset, NJ 08873
(782) 302-1800

New Mexico Restaurant
Association
7800 Marble N.E., Suite 3
Albuquerque, NM 87110
(505) 268-2474

New York State Restaurant
Association
455 New Karner Road
Albany, NY 12205
(518) 452-4222

North Carolina Restaurant
Association
P.O. Box 6528
Raleigh, NC 27628
(919) 782-5022

North Dakota Hospitality
    Association
P.O. Box 428
Bismarck, ND 58502
(701) 223-3313

Ohio Restaurant Association
    1525 Bethel Road,
        Suite 301
    Columbus, OH 43220
    (614) 442-3535

Oklahoma Restaurant Association
    3800 N. Portland Avenue
    Oklahoma City, OK 73112
    (405) 942-8181

Oregon Restaurant Association
    8565 S.W. Salish Lane,
        Suite 120
    Wilsonville, OR 97070
    (503) 682-4422

Pennsylvania Restaurant
    Association
    100 State Street
    Harrisburg, PA 17101
    (717) 232-4433

Rhode Island Hospitality and
    Tourism Association
    1206 Jefferson Boulevard
    Warwick, RI 02886
    (401) 732-4881

Hospitality Association of
    South Carolina
    1338 Main Street,
        Suite 505
    Columbia, SC 29201
    (803) 765-9000

South Dakota Restaurant
    Association
    P.O. Box 638
    Pierre, SD 57501
    (605) 224-5050

Tennessee Restaurant Association
    P.O. Box 681207
    1224-A Lakeview Drive
    Franklin, TN 37068
    (615) 790-2703

Texas Restaurant Association
    1400 Lavaca Street
    Austin, TX 78701
    (512) 472-3666

Utah State Restaurant Association
    141 W. Haven Avenue, Suite 2
    Salt Lake City, UT 84115
    (801) 322-0123

Vermont Lodging and Restaurant
    Association
    3 Main Street,
        Suite 106
    Burlington, VT 05401
    (802) 660-9001

Virginia Hospitality and
    Travel Association
    2101 Libbie Avenue
    Richmond, VA 23230
    (804) 288-3065

Restaurant Association of the
    State of Washington
    2405 Evergreen Park Drive,
        S.W.
    Olympia, WA 98502
    (360) 956-7279

West Virginia Hospitality and
    Travel Association
P.O. Box 2391
Charleston, WV 25328
(304) 342-6511

Wisconsin Restaurant Association
    2801 N. Fish Hatchery Road
    Madison, WI 53711
    (608) 251-3663

Wyoming Lodging and
    Restaurant Association
P.O. Box 1003
Cheyenne, WY 82003
(307) 634-8816

RECRUITERS

The following is a list of companies that can help you obtain a position in the food service industry.

A la Carte International, Inc.
1120 Laskin Road
Virginia Beach, VA 23451
(804) 425-6111

Career Consulting Group, Inc.
1100 Summer Street
Stamford, CT 06905
(203) 975-8808

Robert W. Dingman Co.
32129 W. Lindero Canyon
Road, Suite 206
Westlake Village, CA 91351
(818) 991-5950

Dixie Search Associates
501 Village Trace,
Building 9
Marietta, GA 30067
(770) 850-0250

Dunhill, Inc.
303 W. Main Street
Freehold, NJ 07728
(908) 431-2700

ERP Solutions
45 Whippoorwill Drive
Palmcoast, FL 32184
(904) 447-5820

Elliott Associates, Inc.
104 S. Broadway
Tarrytown, NY 10591
(914) 631-4904

Executive Referral Services, Inc.
8770 W. Bryn Mawr
Chicago, IL 60631
(312) 693-6622

Miriam Factors Employment
Agency
9763 W. Pico Boulevard,
Suite 203
Los Angeles, CA 90035
(213) 553-8677

Ford & Associates
P.O. Box 45
Schnecksville, PA 18078
(610) 760-1122

Franchise Search Inc.
    20 Lattingtown Road
    Glen Cove, NY 11542
    (516) 671-6447

Harper Associates
    29870 Middlebelt
    Farmington Hills, MI 48334
    (810) 932-1170

Hospitality International
    181 Port Watson Street
    Cortland, NY 13045
    (607) 756-8550

Hospitality Resources
        International Ltd.
    14 E. 60th Street, Suite 1210
    New York, NY 10022
    (212) 838-9447

Management Recruiters
        of North Reno
    1350 Stardust, Suite A-5
    Reno, NV 89503
    (702) 787-8009

Management Recruiters
        of Portland
    2020 Lloyd Center
    Portland, OR 97232
    (503) 287-8701

Management Recruiters
        of Wyoming
    3614 U.S. Highway 87
    Banner, WY 82832
    (307) 683-3096

Earl M. McDermid & Associates
    P.O. Box 6202
    Buffalo Grove, IL 60089
    (708) 541-9066

McGuire Executive Search, Inc.
    1650 Sand Lake Road,
        Suite 302
    Orlando, FL 32809
    (407) 857-1600

National Restaurant Search
    910 W. Lake Street,
        Suite 108
    Roselle, IL 60172
    (702) 924-1800

OSS, Inc.
    P.O. Box 2379
    Roundrock, TX 78680
    (512) 255-2424

Wade Palmer & Associates, Inc.
    3830 Pioneer Road
    Rogersville, MO 65742
    (417) 889-3434

ProResources, Inc.
    1801 E. Ninth Street
    Cleveland, OH 44114
    (216) 579-1515

Recruiting Specialists
    P.O. Box 572
    Dedham, MA 02027
    (617) 329-5850

Retail Recruiters
    111 Presidential Boulevard,
        Suite 211
    Bala Cynwyd, PA 19004
    (610) 667-6565

Roth Young Executive
        Recruiters
    4620 W. 77th Street #290
    Minneapolis, MN 55435
    (612) 831-6655

Search Associates
   P.O. Box 10703
   Fort Smith, AR 72917
   (501) 452-0005

Target Search, Inc.
   288 Lancaster Avenue
   Malvern, PA 19355
   (610) 889-2000

APPENDIX C

INDUSTRY TRADE PERIODICALS

Beverage World
226 W. 26th Street
10th Floor
New York, NY
(212) 822-5930

Cheers
Adams Media, Inc.
1180 Avenue of the Americas
New York, NY 10036
(617) 356-7683

Cooking for Profit
CP Publishing, Inc.
104 S. Main Street, 7th Floor
Fond du Lac, WI 54935
(414) 923-3700

Cornell Hotel & Restaurant
    Administration Quarterly
Cornell University
185 Statler Hall
Ithaca, NY 14853
(888) 437-4636

Food Management
Penton Publications
1100 Superior Avenue
Cleveland, OH 44114
(216) 696-7000

Food Review
USDA/ERS-NASS
341 Victory Drive
Herndon, VA 20170
(800) 999-6779

Foodservice Director
Bill Communications
355 Park Avenue S.
New York, NY 10010
(212) 592-6264

Foodservice Equipment and
    Suppliers
Cahners Publishing Co.
8773 S. Ridgeline Boulevard
Highlands Ranch, CO 80126
(303) 470-4000

Hospitality Design
Bill Communications
355 Park Avenue S.
New York, NY 10010
(212) 592-6265

Nation's Restaurant News
Lebhar/Friedman, Inc.
P.O. Box 31179
Tampa, FL 33631
(800) 944-4676

Pasta Journal
National Pasta Association
2101 Wilson Boulevard #920
Arlington, VA 22201
(703) 841-0818

Pizza Today
National Association of
    Pizza Operators
P.O. Box 1347
New Albany, IN 47151
(812) 949-0909

Restaurant Business
Bill Communications
355 Park Avenue S.
New York, NY 10010
(212) 592-6264

Restaurant Economic Trends
National Restaurant
    Association
1200 17th Street, N.W.
Washington, DC 20036
(202) 331-5900

Restaurant Hospitality
Penton Publications
1100 Superior Avenue
Cleveland, OH 44114
(216) 696-7000

Restaurant & Institutions
Cahners Publishing Co.
8773 S. Ridgeline Boulevard
Highlands Ranch, CO 90126
(303) 470-4000

Restaurant USA
National Restaurant
    Association
1200 17th Street, N.W.
Washington, DC 20036
(202) 331-5900

ONE- AND TWO-YEAR SCHOOL PROGRAMS IN HOTEL, RESTAURANT, AND INSTITUTIONAL MANAGEMENT

The following list is arranged alphabetically by state. Additional information for most of the schools listed are available directly from the school, including: number of students enrolled; numbers of faculty members; names of directors of program; costs; and brief program descriptions.

Contact each school for information on its program. Many of the schools listed also may offer four-year and other programs. The prospective student will want to get complete information from each school he or she is considering.

Alabama

Bessemer State Technical
    College
Institutional Foodservice
P.O. Box 308
Bessemer, AL 35021

Carver State Technical
    College
Commercial Foodservice
414 Stanton Street
Mobile, AL 36617

Community College of the
    Air Force
Foodservice and Lodging
CCAF/AYS Building 836
Maxwell AFB, AL 36112

Jefferson State Community
    College
Foodservice Management
    and Technology
2601 Carson Road
Birmingham, AL 35215

Lawson State Community
    College
Commercial Foods
3060 Wilson Road S.W.
Elirmingham, AL 35221

Wallace State Community
    College
Commercial Foods
801 Main Street N.W.
Hanceville, AL 35077-9080

Alaska

Alaska Pacific University
    Travel and Hospitality
        Management
    4101 University Drive
    Anchorage, AK 99508

Alaska Vocational Technical
        Center
    Foodservice Technology
    P.O. Box 889
    Seward, AK 99664

University of Alaska
    Foodservice Technology
    3211 Providence Avenue
    Anchorage, AK 99508

Arizona

Cochise College
    Hotel and Restaurant
        Management Program
    Sierra Vista, AZ 85635

Phoenix College
    Foodservice Administration
    1202 W. Thomas Road
    Phoenix, AZ 85013

Pima County Community
        College District
    Hospitality Department
    P.O. Box 5027,
        1255 N. Stone Avenue
    Tuscon, AZ 85703-0027

Scottsdale Community College
    Hospitality Management/
        Culinary Arts
    9000 East Chaparral Road
    Scottsdale, AZ 85256

Arkansas

Quapaw Vocational Technical
School
Foodservice Program
201 Vo Tech Drive
Hot Springs, AR 71913

North Arkansas College
Hotel and Restaurant
Management Program
Harrison, AR 72601
(501) 743-3000

Southern Arkansas University
Tech
Hotel, Restaurant Department
SAU Tech Station
Camden, AR 71701

California

American River College
Foodservice Management
4700 College Oak Drive
Sacramento, CA 95841

Bakersfield College
Foodservice Program
1801 Panorama Drive
Bakersfield, CA 93305

Cabrillo College
Foodservice Technology
6500 Soquel Drive
Aptos, CA 95003

California Culinary Academy
Culinary Arts/Chef Training
625 Polk Street
San Francisco, CA 94102

Chaffey College
Hotel and Foodservice
Management
5885 Haven Avenue
Rancho Cucamonga, CA
91701

City College of San Francisco
Hotel and Restaurant
Department
50 Phelan Avenue
San Francisco, CA 94112

College of the Canyons
Hotel and Restaurant
Management Program
Santa Clarita, CA 91356

Columbia Community College
Hospitality Management
P.O. Box 1849
Columbia, CA 95310

Contra Costa College
Culinary Arts
2600 Mission Bell Drive
San Pablo, CA 93806

Cypress College
Culinary Arts and Hospitality
Management
9200 Valley View Boulevard
Cypress CA 90630

Diablo Valley College
  Hotel, Restaurant
    Management
  321 Golf Club Road
  Pleasant Hill, CA 94523

El Camino College
  Foodservice Management
  16007 Crenshaw
  Torrance, CA 90506

Glendale Community College
  Foodservice Management
  1500 N. Verdugo Road
  Glendale, CA 91208

Grossmont College
  Foodservice Management
  8800 Grossmont College
    Drive
  El Cajon, CA 92020

ITT Technical Institute,
    San Diego
  Hotel and Restaurant Program
  San Diego, CA 92123

Lake Tahoe Community College
  Innkeeping and Restaurant
    Operations
  P.O. Box 14445
  South Lake Tahoe, CA 95702

Laney College
  Culinary Arts Department
  900 Fallon Street
  Oakland, CA 94607

Long Beach City College
  Hotel and Restaurant
    Management Program
  4901 E. Carson Street
  Long Beach, CA 90808

Los Angeles Trade-Technical
    College
  Chef Training/Restaurant
    Management
  400 W. Washington Boulevard
  Los Angeles, CA 90015

Los Angeles Valley College
  Hotel and Restaurant
    Management Program
  Van Nuys, CA 91401

Merced College
  Foodservice Program
  3600 M Street
  Merced, CA 95348

Mission College
  Hospitality Management
  3000 Mission College
    Boulevard
  Santa Clara, CA 95054

Modesto Junior College
  Foodservice Program
  435 College Avenue
  Modesto, CA 95350

Monterey Peninsula College
  Hotel and Restaurant
    Management Program
  Monterey, CA 93940

Mt. San Antonio College
  Hotel and Restaurant
    Management Program
  Walnut, CA 91789

Orange Coast College
  Hotel Restaurant Management/
    Culinary Arts
  2701 Fairview Road
  Costa Mesa, CA 92626

Oxnard College
Hotel and Restaurant
Management
4000 S. Rose Avenue
Oxnard, CA 93033

Pasadena City College
Foodservice Program
1570 E. Colorado Boulevard
Pasadena, CA 91106

San Diego Mesa College
Foodservice Occupations/
Hotel, Motel Management
7250 Mesa College Drive
San Diego, CA 92111

San Joaquin Delta College
Foodservice Management/
Foodservice Industry
5151 Pacific Avenue
Stockton, CA 95207

Santa Barbara City College
Hotel, Restaurant
Management/Culinary Arts
721 Cliff Drive
Santa Barbara, CA 93109

Santa Rosa Junior College
Hotel and Restaurant
Management Program
1501 Mendocino Avenue
Santa Rosa, CA 95401

Shasta College
Culinary Arts
1065 N. Old Oregon Trail
Redding, CA 96001

Skyline College
Hotel and Restaurant
Operations
3300 College Drive
San Bruno, CA 94066

Victor Valley College
Restaurant Management
18422 Bear Valley Road
Victorville, CA 92392

Yuba Community College
Foodservice Management
2088 N. Beale Road
Marysville, CA 95901

Colorado

Career Development
Center
Restaurant Careers
1200 S. Sunset
Longmont, CO 80501

Colorado Mountain College
Resort Management
Box 5288
Steamboat Springs, CO
80477

Community College of Denver
Hotel and Restaurant
Management Program
P.O. Box 173363
Denver, CO 80217

Denver Institute of Technology
Hospitality Service
Management
7350 N. Broadway
Denver, CO 80221

Emily Griffith Opportunity
School
Food Production Management
and Service
1250 Welton Street
Denver, CO 80204

Mesa State College
Travel, Recreation and
Hospitality Management
Box 2647, 1175 Texas Avenue
Grand Junction, CO 81502

T.H. Pickens Technical Center
Restaurant Arts
500 Buckley Road
Aurora, CO 80011

Pikes Peak Community College
Culinary Arts/Food
Management
5675 S. Academy Boulevard
Colorado Springs, CO 80906

Pueblo Community College
Foodservice Program
900 W. Orman Avenue
Pueblo, CO 81004

Warren Occupational
Technical Center
Restaurant Arts
13300 W. Ellsworth Avenue
Golden, CO 80401

Connecticut

Briarwood College
Hotel, Restaurant Management
2279 Mount Vernon Road
Southington, CT 06489

Manchester Community College
Hotel, Foodservice
Management
60 Bidwell Street
Manchester, CT 06040

Mattatuck Community College
Hospitality Management
750 Chase Parkway
Waterbury, CT 06708

Naugatuck Valley
Community–Technical
College
Hotel and Restaurant
Management Program
705 Chase Parkway
Waterbury, CT 06708
(203) 575-8078

Norwalk Community–Technical
College
Hotel and Restaurant
Management Program
188 Richards Avenue
Norwalk, CT 06854
(203) 857-7060

Three Rivers Community-
Technical College
Hotel and Restaurant
Management Program
Mahan Drive
Norwich, CT 06360
(860) 823-2845

University of New Haven
Hotel, Restaurant, Tourism
Administration
300 Orange Avenue
West Haven, CT 06516

Delaware

Delaware Tech—Southern Campus
  Hospitality Management
  P.O. Box 610
  Georgetown, DE 19947

District of Columbia

Culinary School of Washington,
    Ltd.
  Chef Programs
  1634 I Street NW
  Washington, DC 20006

Florida

Atlantic Vocational Technical
    Center
  Culinary Arts
  4700 N.W. Coconut Creek
    Parkway
  Coconut Creek, FL 33066

Brevard Community College
  Hospitality Management
  1519 Clearlake Road
  Cocoa, FL 32922

Broward Community
    College
  Restaurant Management
  225 E. Las Olas Boulevard
  Fort Lauderdale, FL 33301

Daytona Beach Community
    College
  Hospitality Management
  1200 Volusia Avenue
  Daytona Beach, FL 32115

Florida Community College
    at Jacksonville
  Culinary Arts/Hospitality
    Management
  3939 Roosevelt Boulevard
  Jacksonville, FL 32205

Florida Keys Community College
  Hospitality Management
  5901 W. Junior College Road
  Key West, FL 33040

Gulf Coast Community College
  Hotel, Motel and Restaurant
    Management
  5230 W. Highway 98
  Panama City, FL 32401

Hillsborough Community College
  Hotel and Resort Management/
    Chef Apprentice Training
  P.O. Box 30030
  Tampa, FL 33630

Indian River Community College
Restaurant Management
3209 Virginia Avenue
Fort Pierce, FL 33454

Lake-Sumter Community College
Hotel and Restaurant
Management Program
Leesburg, FL 34788

Manatee Community College
Hospitality Management
5840 26th Street W.
Bradenton, FL 33507

Miami-Dade Community College
Hospitality Management
300 N.E. 2nd Avenue
Miami, FL 33132

Mid-Florida Technical Institute
Commercial Cooking and
Culinary Arts
2900 W. Oakridge Road
Orlando, FL 32809

North Technical Educational
Center
Commercial Foods/
Culinary Arts
7071 Garden Road
Riviera Beach, FL 33404

Okaloosa-Walton Community
College
Commercial Foods
100 College Boulevard
Niceville, FL 32578

Palm Beach Community College
Hospitality Management
4200 S. Congress Avenue
Lake Worth, FL 33461

Pensacola Junior College
Hospitality Management
1000 College Boulevard
Pensacola, FL 32504-8998

PETEC-Clearwater Campus
Culinary Arts
6100 154th Avenue North
Clearwater, FL 34620

Sarasota County Vocational
Technical Center
Commercial Cooking/
Culinary Arts
4748 Beneva Road
Sarasota, FL 34233

Seminole Community College
Culinary Arts/Restaurant
Management
100 Weldon Boulevard
Sanford, FL 32773

St. Augustine Technical
Center
Commercial Foods/
Culinary Arts
2960 Collins Avenue
St. Augustine, FL 32084

Valencia Community College
Hospitality Management
P.O. Box 3028
Orlando, FL 32802

Washington-Holmes Area
Vocational Technical
Center
Commercial Foods and
Culinary Arts
209 Hoyt Street
Chipley, FL 32428

Webber College
  Hotel and Restaurant
    Management
  1201 Alternate Highway
  27 South
  Babson Park, FL 33827

Georgia

Albany Technical Institute
  Culinary Arts
  1021 Lowe Road
  Albany, GA 30310

Atlanta Technical Institute
  Culinary Arts
  1560 Stewart Avenue, S.W.
  Atlanta, GA 30310

Augusta Technical Institute
  Culinary Arts
  3116 Deans Bridge Road
  Augusta, GA 30906

Ben Hill-Irwin Technical Institute
  Culinary Arts
  P.O. Box 1069
  Fitzgerald, GA 31750

Gainesville College
  Hotel, Restaurant and Travel
  P.O. Box 1358
  Gainesville, GA 30503

Gwinnett Technical Institute
  Hotel, Restaurant, Travel
    Management
  P.O. Box 1505,
    1250 Atkinson Road
  Lawrenceville, GA 30246

Macon Technical Institute
  Culinary Arts
  3300 Macon Tech Drive
  Macon, GA 31206

Middle Georgia Technical
    Institute
  Culinary Arts
  1311 Corder Road
  Warner Robins, GA 31088

Savannah Technical Institute
  Culinary Arts
  5717 White Bluff Road
  Savannah, GA 31499

Hawaii

Hawaii Community College
  Foodservice Program
  1175 Manono Street
  Hilo, HI 96720-4091

Leeward Community College
  Foodservice Program
  96-045 Ala Ike
  Pearl City, HI 96782

University of Hawaii—Kapiolani
    Community College
    Foodservice and Hospitality
       Education
    4303 Diamond Head Road
    Honolulu, HI 96816

University of Hawaii—Maui
    Community College
    Foodservice Program
    310 Kaahumanu Avenue
    Kahului, HI 96732

Idaho

Boise State University
    Culinary Arts
    1910 University Drive
    Boise, ID 83725

College of Southern Idaho
    Hotel, Restaurant Management
    P.O. Box 1238
    Twin Falls, ID 83303

Ricks College
    Restaurant and Catering
       Management
    Clarke Building
    Rexburg, ID 83440

Illinois

Black Hawk College
    Hotel and Restaurant
       Management Program
    Moline, IL 61265

Chicago Hospitality Institute
    Foodservice Administration,
       Hotel, Motel
       Management
    226 W. Jackson Boulevard
    Chicago, IL 60606

City Colleges of Chicago
    Harold Washington
       College
    Hotel and Restaurant
       Management Program
    30 E. Lake Street
    Chicago, IL 60601

College of DuPage
    Hospitality Administration
    22nd Street and
       Lambert Road
    Glen Ellyn, IL 60137

College of Lake County
    Foodservice Management/
       Culinary Arts
    19351 W. Washington
    Grayslake, IL 60030

The Cooking and Hospitality
       Institute of Chicago
    Professional Cooking/
       Hospitality Management
    361 W. Chestnut
    Chicago, IL 60610

Elgin Community College
Culinary Arts/Hospitality
Management
1700 Spartan Drive
Elgin, IL 60123

William Rainey Harper
Community College
Foodservice Management/
Culinary Arts
1200 W. Algonquin Road
Palatine, IL 60067

Joliet Junior College
Culinary Arts/Hotel
Restaurant Management
1216 Houbolt
Joliet, IL 60436

Kendall College
Culinary Arts/Hospitality
Management
2408 Orrington Avenue
Evanston, IL 60201

Kennedy-King College
Food Management
6800 S. Wentworth
Avenue
Chicago, IL 60621

Lewis & Clark Community
College
Hospitality Industry
Programs
5800 Godfrey Road
Godfrey, IL 62035

Lexington Institute
Hospitality Careers
10840 S. Western Avenue
Chicago, IL 60643

Lincoln Trail College
Foodservice Technology
Route #3
Robinson, IL 62454

MacCormac College
Hotel and Restaurant
Management Program
506 S. Wabash Avenue
Chicago, IL 60605

Moraine Valley Community
College
Restaurant Management
10900 S. 88th Avenue
Palos Hill, IL 60465

Oakton Community College
Hotel Management
1600 E. Golf Road
Des Plaines, IL 60016

Parkland Community College
Hospitality Industries
2400 W. Bradley
Champaign, IL 61821

Sauk Valley Community College
Foodservice Program
173 Illinois Route 2
Dixon, IL 61021

Triton College
Hospitality Institute
2000 Fifth Avenue
River Grove, EL 60171

Washburne Trade School
Chefs Training
3233 W. 31st Street
Chicago, IL 60623

Indiana

Ball State University
  Foodservice Management
  Practical Arts Building
  Muncie, IN 47306

Indiana-Purdue University
    at Indianapolis
  Restaurant, Hotel
    and Institutional
    Management
  799 W. Michigan Street
  Indianapolis, IN 46202

Ivy Tech State College
  Culinary Arts
  5727 Sohl Avenue
  Hammond, IN 46320

Ivy Tech State College
  Hotel and Restaurant
    Administration/Culinary
  P.O. Box 1763
  Indianapolis, IN 46206

Purdue University
  Restaurant, Hotel and
    Institutional Management
  106 Stone Hall
  West Lafayette, IN 47907

Vincennes University
  Hospitality Management/
    Culinary Arts
  1002 N. 1st Street
  Vincennes, IN 47591

Iowa

American Institute of Commerce
  Hotel and Restaurant
    Management Program
  Davenport, IA 52807

Des Moines Area Community
    College
  Hospitality Careers
  2006 Ankeny Boulevard
  Ankeny, IA 50021

Indian Hills Community College
  Foodservice/Cooking
  525 Grandview
  Ottumwa, IA 52501

Iowa Lakes Community College
  Hotel, Motel and Restaurant
    Management
  3200 College Drive
  Emmetsburg, IA 50536

Iowa Western Community
    College
  Culinary Arts
  2100 College Road, Box 4-C
  Council Bluffs, IA 51502

Kirkwood Community College
  Restaurant Management/
    Culinary Arts
  6301 Kirkwood Boulevard
    S.W.
  Cedar Rapids, IA 52406

Kansas

Butler County Community
    College
    Hotel and Restaurant
        Management Program
    El Dorado, KS 67042

Central College
    Foodservice Management
    1200 S. Main
    McPherson, KS 67460

Cloud County Community
    College
    Hospitality Management
    2221 Campus Drive
    Concordia, KS 66901

Cowley County Community
        College and
        Vocational–Technical
        School
    Hotel and Restaurant
        Management Program
    Arkansas City, KS 67005

Flint Hills Area Vocational
    Technical School
    Culinary Arts
    3301 W. 18th Avenue
    Emporia, KS 66801

Hesston College
    Hotel, Restaurant,
        Institutional Management
    Box 3000
    Hesston, KS 67072

Johnson County Community
    College
    Hospitality Program
    12345 College
    Overland Park, KS 66210

Kansas City Area Vocational
    Technical School
    Commercial Foodservice
    2220 N. 59th Street
    Kansas City, KS 66104

Kaw Area Vocational Technical
    Institute
    Foodservice Program
    5724 Huntoon
    Topeka, KS 66604

Northeast Kansas Area Vocational
    Technical School
    Quantity Foods
    1501 W. Riley
    Atchison, KS 66002

Salina Area Vocational
    Technical School
    Foodservice Management
    2562 Scanlan
    Salina, KS 67401

Wichita Area Vocational
    Technical School
    Food Service
    Mid-management and
        Commercial Cooking
    324 N. Emporia
    Wichita, KS 67202

Kentucky

Daviess County State Vocational
    Technical School
    Commercial Foods
    1901 S.E. Parkway
    Owensboro, KY 42303

Elizabethtown State Technical
    School
    Commercial Foods
    505 University Drive
    Elizabethtown, KY 42701

Jefferson Community College
    Culinary Arts
    109 E. Broadway
    Louisville, KY 40202

Sullivan College
    Culinary Arts/Hotel,
        Restaurant Management
    3101 Bardstown Road
    Louisville, KY 40205

West Kentucky State Vocational
    Technical School
    Culinary Arts
    P.O. Box 7408
    Paducah, KY 42001

Louisiana

Baton Rouge Vocational
    Technical Institute
    Culinary Occupations
    3250 N. Acadian
        Throughway
    Baton Rouge, LA 70805

Sidney N. Collier Vocational
    Technical School
    Culinary Occupations
    3727 Louisa Street
    New Orleans, LA 70126

Delgado Community College
    Culinary Apprenticeship
        Program
    615 City Park Avenue
    New Orleans, LA 70119

New Orleans Regional
    Vocational Technical
        Institute
    Culinary Arts
    980 Navarre Avenue
    New Orleans, LA 70124

Nicholls State University
    Food Management
    P.O. Box 2014
    Thibodaux, LA 70310

Southern University
    Hotel, Motel, Restaurant
        Management
    3050 Martin Luther King Drive
    Shreveport, LA 71107

Maine

Eastern Maine Technical College
Food Management/
Food Technology
354 Hogan Road
Bangor, ME 04401

Southern Maine Technical
College
Hotel, Motel and Restaurant
Management and
Culinary Arts
Fort Road
South Portland, ME 04106

Washington County Technical
College
Foodservice Program
River Road
Calais, ME 04619

York County Technical College
Hotel and Restaurant
Management Program
Wells, ME 04090

Maryland

Allegany Community College
Foodservice Management
Willow Brook Road
Cumberland, MD 21502

Anne Arundel Community
College
Hotel, Restaurant Management
101 College Parkway C-205
Arnold, MD 21012

Baltimore's International
Culinary College
Culinary Arts/Restaurant
Management
19-21 South Gay Street
Baltimore, MD 21202

Essex Community College
Hotel, Motel, Restaurant,
Club Management
7201 Rossville Boulevard
Baltimore County, MD 21237

Hagerstown Junior College
Hospitality Industry
751 Robinwood Drive
Hagerstown, MD 21740

Howard Community College
Culinary
Apprenticeship/Restaurant
Management
10920 Route 108
Ellicott City, MD 21043

Montgomery College
Hospitality Management
51 Mannakee Street
Rockville, MD 20850

Prince George's Community
College
Hospitality Services
Management
301 Largo Road
Largo, MD 20772

Wor-Wic Tech Community
    College
    Hotel, Motel, Restaurant
    Management
    Route 3, Box 79
    Berlin, MD 21811

Massachusetts

Bay State College
    Hotel and Hospitality
        Management
    122 Commonwealth Avenue
    Boston, MA 02116

Becker Junior College
    Resort, Hotel, Restaurant
        Management
    3 Paxton Street
    Keicester, MA 01524

Berkshire Community College
    Hotel and Restaurant
        Management
    West Street
    Pittsfield, MA 01201

Bunker Hill Community College
    Hotel, Restaurant, Travel
        Management
    New Rutherford Avenue
    Boston, MA 02129

Cape Cod Community College
    Hotel, Restaurant Management
    Route 132
    West Barnstable, MA 02668

Endicott College
    Hotel, Restaurant, and Travel
        Administration
    376 Hale Street
    Beverly, MA 01915

Katharine Gibbs School
    Hotel, Restaurant
        Management
    5 Arlington Street
    Boston, MA 02116

Holyoke Community College
    Hospitality Management
    303 Homestead Avenue
    Holyoke, MA 01040

Massachusetts Bay Community
        College
    Hospitality Management
    Fay Road
    Framingham, MA 01701

Massasoit Community
        College
    Culinary Arts
    1 Massasoit Boulevard
    Brockton, MA 02402

Middlesex Community College
    Hotel and Restaurant
        Management Program
    33 Kearney Square
    Lowell, MA 01852

Mount Ida College
    Hotel, Institution
        Management
    777 Dedham Street
    Newton Center, MA 02159

Newbury College
Hospitality Management and
Culinary Arts
129 Fisher Avenue
Brookline, MA 02146

Northeastern University
Hotel and Restaurant
Management/Culinary Arts
270 Ryder Building
Boston, MA 02115

Northern Essex Community
College
Hotel and Restaurant
Management Program
Haverhill, MA 01830

Quincy Junior College
Hospitality Management
34 Coddington Street
Quincy, MA 02169

Quinsigamond Community
College
Hotel and Restaurant
Management
670 W. Boylston Street
Worcester, MA 01606-2092

Michigan

Bay Mills Community College
Hotel and Restaurant
Management Program
Brimley, MI 49715

Davenport College of Business
Restaurant and Lodging
Management
415 E. Fulton
Grand Rapids, MI 49507

Ferris State University
Foodservice Hospitality
Management
901 S. State Street
Big Rapids, MI 49307

Henry Ford Community
College
Hospitality Studies
5101 Evergreen
Dearborn, MI 48128

Gogebic Community College
Foodservice and Hospitality
Management
E4946 Jackson Road
Ironwood, MI 49938

Grand Rapids Junior College
Culinary Arts, Food and
Beverage Management
143 Bostwick, N.E.
Grand Rapids, MI 49503

Kalamazoo Valley Community
College
Foodservice Management
6767 W. O Avenue
Kalamazoo, MI 49009

Lake Michigan College
Food Management
2755 E. Napier
Benton Harbor, MI 49022

Lansing Community College
  Hospitality Systems
  419 N. Capital Avenue
  Lansing, MI 48901

Macomb Community College
  Culinary Arts/ Professional
      Foodservice
  44575 Garfield Road
  Mount Clemens, MI 48044

Mott Community College
  Foodservice Management/
      Culinary Arts
  1401 East Court Street
  Flint, MI 48503

Muskegon Community College
  Foodservice, Lodging and
  Travel Management
  221 S. Quarterfine Road
  Muskegon, MI 49442

Northern Michigan University
  Restaurant Foods
  Jacobetti Center, Route 550
  Marquette, MI 49855

Northwestern Michigan College
  Foodservice and Hospitality
      Management
  1701 E. Front Street
  Traverse City, MI 49684

Northwood Institute
  Hotel, Restaurant Management
  3225 Cook Road
  Midland, MI 48640

Oakland Community College
  Hospitality Management/
      Culinary Arts
  27055 Orchard Lake Road
  Farmington Hills, MI 48018

People's Community Civic
      League
  Culinary Arts
  5961 14th Street
  Detroit, MI 48208

Schoolcraft College
  Culinary Arts and Culinary
      Management
  18600 Haggerty Road
  Livonia, MI 48152

Siena Heights College
  Hotel, Restaurant and
      Instituional Management
  1247 E. Siena Heights Drive
  Adrian, MI 49221

State Technical Institute
  Culinary Arts
  Alber Drive
  Plainwell, MI 49080

Suomi College
  Hotel, Restaurant Management
  601 Quincy Street
  Hancock, MI 49930

Washtenaw Community College
  Culinary Arts/Hospitality
      Management
  4800 E. Huron River Drive
  Ann Arbor, MI 48106

Wayne County Community
      College
  Culinary Arts
  8551 Greenfield
  Detroit, MI 48228

West Shore Community College
  Foodservice Management
  3000 Stiles Road
  Scottville, MI 49454

Minnesota

Alexandria Technical College
  Hotel, Restaurant Management
  1601 Jefferson
  Alexandria, MN 56308

Dakota County Technical College
  Foodservice Management
  1300 E. 145th Street
  Rosemount, MN 55068

Detroit Lakes Technical College
  Chef Training and
      Commercial Cooking
  East Highway 34
  Detroit Lakes, MN 56501

Duluth Technical College
  Culinary Arts/Restaurant
      Management
  2101 Trinity Road
  Duluth, MN 55811

Hennepin Technical College
  Cook/Chef
  9000 Brooklyn Boulevard
  Brooklyn Park, MN 55445

Mankato Technical College
  Culinary Arts
  1920 Lee Boulevard
  North Mankato, MN 56001

Minneapolis Technical College
  Culinary Arts/Hospitality
      Management
  1415 Hennepin Avenue
  Minneapolis, MN 55403

Moorhead Technical College
  Chef Training
  1900 28th Avenue South
  Moorhead, MN 56560

Normandale Community College
  Hospitality Management
  9700 France Avenue S.
  Bloomington, MN 55431

Northeast Metro Technical
      College
  Quantity Foods/Chef Training
  3300 Century Avenue N.
  White Bear Lake, MN 55110

Rainy River Community College
  Hotel and Restaurant
      Management Program
  International Falls, MN 56649

Southwestern Technical College
  Foodservice Department
  North Hiawatha Avenue
  Pipestone, MN 56164

St. Paul Technical College
  Restaurant and Hotel Cookery
  235 Marshall Avenue
  St. Paul, MN 55102

University of Minnesota,
      Crookston
  Hospitality Department
  Highways 2 and 75 North
  Crookston, MN 56716

Mississippi

Copiah-Lincoln Community
College, Natchez
Hotel and Restaurant
Management Program
Natchez, MS 39120

East Mississippi Community
College
Hotel and Restaurant
Management Program
P.O. Box 158
Scooba, MS 39358

Hinds Community College
Hotel, Restaurant
Management Technology
3925 Sunset Drive
Jackson, MS 39213

Meridian Community College
Restaurant and Hotel
Management
5500 Highway 19 North
Meridian, MS 39307

Mississippi Gulf Coast
Community College
Motel, Restaurant Technology
2226 Switzer Road
Gulfport, MS 39507

Northeast Mississippi
Community College
Hotel, Restaurant
Management Technology
Cunningham Boulevard
Booneville, MS 38829

Northwest Mississippi
Community College
Hotel and Restaurant
Management Program
Senatobia, MS 38668

Missouri

Crowder College
Hospitality Management
601 Laclede
Neosho, MO 64850

East Central College
Hotel and Restaurant
Management Program
Union, MO 63084

Jefferson College
Hotel, Restaurant Management
P.O. Box 1000
Hillsboro, MO 63050

Penn Valley Community College
Lodging and Foodservice
Management/Culinary Arts
3201 Southwest Trafficway
Kansas City, MO 64152

St. Louis Community College
at Forest Park
Hospitality Restaurant
Management
5600 Oakland Avenue
St. Louis, MO 63110

Montana

Missoula Vocational Technical
    Center
Commercial Food Production
909 South Avenue West
Missoula, MT 59801

Nebraska

Central Community College
    Hotel, Motel, Restaurant
        Management
    P.O. Box 1024
    Hastings, NE 68901

Metropolitan Community College
    Foodservice Technology
    P.O. Box 3777, 30th and Fort
        Streets
    Omaha, NE 68103

Nebraska College of Business
    Hotel, Restaurant Management
    3636 California Street
    Omaha, NE 68131

Southeast Community College
    Foodservice Program
    8800 O Street
    Lincoln, NE 68520

Nevada

Clark County Community
    College
    Hotel, Restaurant, Casino
        Management and Culinary
        Arts
    3200 E. Cheyenne Avenue
    North Las Vegas, NV 89030

Community College of
    Southern Nevada
    Hotel and Restaurant
        Management Program
    North Las Vegas, NV 89030

Truckee Meadows Community
    College
    Foodservice Techniques
    7000 Dandini Boulevard
    Reno, NV 89512

New Hampshire

Hesser College
    Hotel, Restaurant Management
    25 Fowell Street
    Manchester, NH 03101

New Hampshire College
    Hotel, Restaurant
        Management and
        Culinary Arts
    2500 N. River Road
    Manchester, NH 03104

New Hampshire Technical
        College
    Culinary Arts
    2020 Riverside Drive
    Berlin, NH 03570

University of New Hampshire
    Foodservice Management
    Barton Hall, Room 105
    Durham, NH 03824

New Jersey

Atlantic Community College
    Culinary Arts/Hospitality
        Management
    Black Horse Pike
    Mays Landing, NJ 08330

Bergen Community College
    Hotel, Restaurant Management
    400 Paramus Road
    Paramus, NJ 07652

Brookdale Community College
    Foodservice Management
    Newman Springs Road
    Lincroft, NJ 07738

Burlington County College
    Hospitality Management
    Route 530
    Pemberton, NJ 08068

Camden County College
    Food Management
    Little Gloucester Road,
        Box 200
    Blackwood, NJ 08012

Cape May County Vocational
        Technical Schools
    Foods Production/
        Culinary Arts
    Crest Haven Road
    Cape May Court House,
        NJ 08210

County College of Morris
    Hotel, Restaurant Management
    Center Grove Road
    Randolph, NJ 07869

Essex County College
    Hotel and Restaurant
        Management Program
    303 University Avenue
    Newark, NJ 07102

Hudson County Community
        College
    Culinary Arts
    161 Newkirk Street
    Jersey City, NJ 07306

Mercer County Community
　College
　Hotel, Restaurant and
　　Institution Management
　1200 Old Trenton Road
　Trenton, NJ 08690

Middlesex County College
　Hotel, Restaurant and
　　Institution Management
　155 Mill Road, Box 3050
　Edison, NJ 08818

Ocean County College
　Foodservice Management
　College Drive
　Toms River, NJ 08753

Raritan Valley Community
　College
　Hotel and Restaurant
　　Management Program
　P.O. Box 3300
　Somerville, NJ 08876

Union County College
　Hotel and Restaurant
　　Management Program
　Cranford, NJ 07016

New Mexico

Albuquerque Technical
　　Vocational Institute
　Culinary Arts
　525 Buena Vista S.E.
　Albuquerque, NM 87059

Santa Fe Community College
　Hotel and Restaurant
　　Management Program
　Santa Fe, NM 87502

New York

Adirondack Community College
　Foodservice Program
　Bay Road
　Queensbury, NY 12804

Berkeley College
　Hotel and Restaurant
　　Management Program
　White Plains, NY 10604

Broome Community College
　Hotel and Restaurant
　　Management Program
　Binghamton, NY 13902

Bryant & Stratton
　　Business Institute
　Hotel and Restaurant
　　Management Program
　Albany, NY 12205

Community College of the
　　Finger Lakes
　Hotel and Resort Management
　Lincoln Hill
　Canandaigua, NY 14424

Culinary Institute of America
  Culinary Arts
  Route 9
  Hyde Park, NY 12538

Erie Community College North
  Foodservice Administration/
    Restaurant Management
  Main and Youngs Road
  Buffalo, NY 14221

Finger Lakes Community College
  Hotel and Restaurant
    Management Program
  Canandaigua, NY 14424

Fulton Montgomery Community
    College
  Foodservice Administration
  Route 67
  Johnstown, NY 12866

Genesee Community College
  Hospitality Management
  One College Road
  Batavia, NY 14020

Jefferson Community College
  Hospitality and Tourism
    Management
  Outer Coffeen Street
  Watertown, NY 13601

LaGuardia Community College
  Commercial Foodservice
    Management
  31-10 Thomson Avenue
  Long Island City, NY 11101

Mohawk Valley Community
    College
  Foodservice Program
  Upper Floyd Avenue
  Rome, NY 13440

Monroe Community College
  Food, Hotel and Tourism
    Managment
  1000 E. Henrietta Road
  Rochester, NY 14623

Nassau Community College
  Hotel and Restaurant
    Management
  Building K
  Garden City, NY 11530

New York City Technical
    College
  Hotel and Restaurant
    Management
  300 Jay Street
  Brooklyn, NY 11201

New York Food and Hotel
    Management School
  Hospitality Management
  154 W. 14th Street
  New York, NY 10011

New York Institute of Technology
  Culinary Arts
  Carleton Avenue
  Central Islip, NY 11722-4597

New York Restaurant School
  Culinary Arts/Restaurant
    Management
  27 W. 34th Street
  New York, NY 10001

Niagara County Community
    College
  Professional Chef
  3111 Saunders
    Settlement Road
  Sanborn, NY 14132

Onondaga Community College
Foodservice Administration/
Hotel Technology
Route 173
Syracuse, NY 13215

Paul Smith's College
Hotel Restaurant Management/
Culinary Arts
Paul Smiths, NY 12970

Rockland Community College
Foodservice Management
145 College Road
Suffern, NY 10901

Schenectady County
Community College
Hotel, Culinary Arts and
Tourism
78 Washington Avenue
Schenectady, NY 12305

State University of New York
at Alfred
Foodservice Department
South Brooklyn Avenue
Wellsville, NY 14895

State University of New York
at Canton
Hotel and Restaurant
Management
Cornell Drive
Canton, NY 13617

State University of New York
at Cobleskill
Foodservice and Hospitality
Administration
Champlin Hall
Cobleskill, NY 12043

State University of New York
at Delhi
Hospitality Management
Alumni Hall
Delhi, NY 13753

State University of New York
at Farmingdale
Restaurant Management
Melville Road, Thompson Hall
Farmingdale, NY 11735

State University of New York
at Morrisville
Food Administration,
Restaurant Management
Bailey Annex
Morrisville, NY 13408

Suffolk County Community
College
Hotel, Restaurant Management
Speonk-Riverhead Road
Riverhead, NY 11901

Sullivan County Community
College
Hospitality Program
Leroy Road
Loch Sheldrake, NY 12759

Tompkins Cortland
Community College
Restaurant Management
170 N. Street
Dryden, NY 13053

Trocaire College
Hotel and Restaurant
Management Program
110 Red Jacket Parkway
Buffalo, NY 14220

Villa Maria College of Buffalo
Foodservice Management
240 Pine Ridge Road
Buffalo, NY 14225

Westchester Community College
Restaurant Management
75 Grasslands Road
Valhalla, NY 10595

North Carolina

Alamance Community College
Foodservice Management
P.O. Box 623
Haw River, NC 27258

Asheville-Buncombe Technical
College
Hospitality Management
Administration/
Culinary Arts
340 Victoria Road
Asheville, NC 28804

Cape Fear Community College
Hotel and Restaurant
Management Program
411 N. Front Street
Wilmington, NC 28401

Central Piedmont Community
College
Hotel, Restaurant Management
P.O. Box 35009
Charlotte, NC 28235

Fayetteville Technical
Community College
Foodservice Management
P.O. Box 35236
Fayetteville, NC 28303

Guilford Technical Community
College
Culinary Arts Technology
P.O. Box 309
Jamestown, NC 27282

Lenoir Community College
Foodservice Management
P.O. Box 188
Kinston, NC 28502

Sandhills Community College
Hotel and Restaurant
Management Program
Pinehurst, NC 28374

Southwestern Community
College
Foodservice Management
275 Webster Road
Sylva, NC 28779

Wake Technical Community
College
Hotel, Restaurant
Management and
Culinary Arts
9101 Fayetteville Road
Raleigh, NC 27603

Wilkes Community College
Hotel, Restaurant Management
Drawer 120
Wilkesboro, NC 28697

North Dakota

Bismarck State College
  Hotel, Restaurant
    Management
  1500 Edwards Avenue
  Bismarck, ND 58501

North Dakota State College
    of Science
  Chef Training and
    Management Technology
  North 6th Street
  Wahpeton, ND 58076

Ohio

Bryant and Stratton College
  Hotel and Restaurant
    Management Program
  Parma, OH 44130

Cincinnati Technical College
  Hotel, Restaurant
    Management/
    Chef Program
  3520 Central Parkway
  Cincinnati, OH 45223

Clermont College of the
    University of Cincinnati
  Hospitality Management
    Technology
  College Drive
  Batavia, OH 45103

Columbus State Community
    College
  Hospitality Management
  550 E. Spring Street
  Columbus, OH 43215

Cuyahoga Community College
  Hospitality Management
  2900 Community College
    Avenue
  Cleveland, OH 44115

Hocking Technical College
  Hotel, Restaurant
    Management/
    Culinary Arts
  Hocking Parkway
  Nelsonville, OH 45764

Jefferson Technical College
  Foodservice Management
  4000 Sunset Boulevard
  Steubenville, OH 43952

North Central Technical
    College
  Hotel and Restaurant
    Management Program
  P.O. Box 698
  Mansfield, OH 44901

Owens Technical College
  Hospitality Management
  P.O. Box 10,000 Oregon
    Road
  Toledo, OH 43699

Sinclair Community College
  Hotel and Restaurant
    Management Program
  444 W. Third Street
  Dayton, OH 45402

Tiffin University
  Hotel and Restaurant
    Management
  155 Miami Street
  Tiffin, OH 44883

University of Akron
  Hotel, Motel, Restaurant
    Management/Culinary Arts
  200 E. Exchange Street
  Akron, OH 44325

University of Toledo Community
    and Technical College
  Foodservice Management/
    Culinary Arts
  Scott Park Campus
  Toledo, OH 43606

Youngstown State University
  Hospitality Management
  410 Wick Avenue
  Youngstown, OH 44555

Oklahoma

Carl Albert State College
  Hotel and Restaurant
    Management
    Program
  Poteau, OK 74953

Great Plains Areas Vocational
    Technical Center
  Foodservice Management
  4500 W. Lee Boulevard
  Lawton, OK 73505

Indian Meridian Vocational
    Technical School
  Commercial Food
    Production
  1312 S. Sangre Road
  Stillwater, OK 74074

Oklahoma State University,
    Technical Branch
  Foodservice Management,
    Culinary Arts
  4th and Mission
  Okmulgee, OK 74447

Pioneer Area Vocational
    Technical School
  Commercial Foods
  2101 N. Ash
  Ponca City, OK 74601

Southern Oklahoma Area
    Vocational Technical Center
  Culinary Arts
  Route #1, Box 14M
  Ardmore, OK 73401

Oregon

Central Oregon Community
    College
  Hotel, Restaurant Management
  2600 N.W. College Way
  Bend, OR 97701

Chemeketa Community College
  Hospitality Systems
  P.O. Box 14007, 4000
  Lancaster Drive N.E.
  Salem, OR 97309

Lane Community College
Hospitality/Culinary Arts
4000 E. 30th Avenue
Eugene, OR 97405

Linn-Benton Community College
Culinary Arts and
Hospitality Services
6500 S.W. Pacific Boulevard
Albany, OR 97321

Mt. Hood Community College
Hospitality and Tourism
26000 S.E. Stark
Gresham, OR 97030

Portland Community College
Hospitality Program
P.O. Box 19000
Portland, OR 97219-0990

Western Culinary Institute
Culinary Arts
1316 S.W. 13th Avenue
Portland, OR 97201

Pennsylvania

Bucks County Community
College
Hotel Restaurant
Management, Chef
Apprenticeship
Swamp Road
Newtown, PA 18940

Butler County Community
College
Restaurant and Foodservice
Management
P.O. Box 1203,
College Drive
Butler, PA 16003-1203

Central Pennsylvania
Business School
Hotel, Motel Management
College Hill Road
Summerdale, PA 17093-0309

Community College of
Allegheny County
Hospitality Management
595 Beatty Road
Monroeville, PA 15146

Community College
of Philadelphia
Hotel, Restaurant and
Institutional Management/
Chef Apprenticeship
1700 Spring Garden
Street
Philadelphia, PA 19130

Delaware County Community
College
Hotel, Restaurant
Management
Route 252
Media, PA 19063

Harcum Junior College
  Hospitality, Tourism Program
  Morris and Montgomery
      Avenues
  Bryn Mawr, PA 19010

Harrisburg Area Community
      College
  Hotel, Restaurant and
      Institutional Management
  3300 Cameron Street
  Harrisburg, PA 17110

Keystone Junior College
  Hospitality Management
  Box 50
  La Plume, PA 18440-0200

Lehigh County Community
      College
  Hotel, Restaurant Management
  2370 Main Street
  Schnecksville, PA 18078

Luzerne County Community
      College
  Hotel, Restaurant Management
  Prospect Street and
      Middle Road
  Nanticoke, PA 18634

Montgomery County
      Community College
  Hotel, Restaurant Management
  340 DeKalb Pike
  Bluebell, PA 19422

Mount Aloysius Junior
      College
  Hotel, Restaurant Management
  William Penn Highway
  Cresson, PA 16630

Northampton Community College
  Restaurant Management
  3835 Green Pond Road
  Bethlehem, PA 18017

Pierce Junior College
  Hospitality Management
  1420 Pine Street
  Philadelphia, PA 19102

Pennsylvania School
      of Technology
  Food and Hospitality
      and Culinary Arts
  One College Avenue
  Williamsport, PA 17701

Pennsylvania State University,
      Beaver Campus
  Hotel and Restaurant
      Management Program
  Monaca, PA 15061

Pennsylvania State University,
      Berks Campus
  Hotel, Restaurant, and
      Institutional Management
  P.O. Box 7009
  Reading, PA 19610-6009

Pittsburgh Technical Institute
  Hotel and Restaurant
      Management Program
  635 Smithfield Street
  Pittsburgh, PA 15222

The Restaurant School
  Restaurant Management/
      Chef Training
  2129 Walnut Street
  Philadelphia, PA 19103

Westmoreland County
    Community College
    Foodservice, Hotel, Motel
      Management/Culinary Arts
    College Station Road
    Youngwood, PA 15697-1895

Widener University
    Hotel and Restaurant
      Management
    13th Street
    Chester, PA 19103

Rhode Island

Johnson & Wales University
    Hospitality Management/
      Culinary Arts
    8 Abbott Park Place
    Providence, RI 02903

Rhode Island School of Design
    Culinary Arts Apprenticeship
    2 College Street
    Providence, RI 02903

South Carolina

Anderson College
    Hotel, Restaurant
      and Tourism
    316 Boulevard
    Anderson, SC 29621

Greenville Technical College
    Foodservice Management
    P.O. Box 5616, Station B
    Greenville, SC 29606-5616

Horry Georgetown
    Technical College
    Hotel, Restaurant
      Management
    P.O. Box 1966,
      Route 501 East
    Conway, SC 29526

Johnson & Wales University
    at Charleston
    Culinary Education,
      Hospitality Department
    701 E. Bay Street
    Charleston, SC 29403

Technical College of the
    Lowcountry
    Hotel, Motel and Restaurant
      Management
    P.O. Box 1288,
      100 S. Rabiut Road
    Beaufort, SC 29901

Trident Technical College
    Hospitality Department
    P.O. Box 10367, HT-P
    Charleston, SC 29411

South Dakota

Black Hills State University
Travel Industry
Management
1200 University
Spearfish, SD 57783

Mitchell Vocational Technical
Institute
Chef Training
821 North Capital
Mitchell, SD 57301

Tennessee

Chattanooga State Technical
Community College
Hotel and Restaurant
Management
Chattanooga, TN 37406

Knoxville State Area
Vocational School
Foodservice Program
1100 Liberty Street
Knoxville, TN 37919

Memphis Culinary Academy
Professional Culinary Arts
1252 Peabody Avenue
Memphis, TN 38104

Pellissippi State Technical
Community College
Hotel and Restaurant
Management Program
Knoxville, TN 37933

State Technical Institute
at Memphis
Hotel, Restaurant Management
5983 Macon Cove
Memphis, TN 38134

Texas

Austin Community College
Hotel and Restaurant
Management Program
5930 Middle Fiskville Road
Austin, TX 78752

Central Texas College
Foodservice Management
P.O. Box 1800
Killeen, TX 76540

Collin County Community
College
Hotel and Restaurant
Management Program
2200 W. University Drive
McKinney, TX 75070

Del Mar College
Restaurant Management
Department
Baldwin at Ayers
Corpus Christi, TX 78404

El Centro College
Food and Hospitality
Services
Main at Lamar
Dallas, TX 75202

El Paso Community College
Hospitality Travel Services
P.O. Box 20500
El Paso, TX 79995

Galveston College
Foodservice Management/
Culinary Arts
4015 Avenue Q
Galveston, TX 77550

Houston Community
College
Hotel, Restaurant
Management/
Culinary Arts
1300 Holman
Houston, TX 77004

Lamar University
Restaurant and Institutional
Food Management
P.O. Box 10035
Beaumont, TX 77710

Laredo Community College
Hotel and Restaurant
Management Program
West End Washington Street
Laredo, TX 78040

Le Chef Culinary Arts School
Culinary Arts
6020 Dillard Circle
Austin, TX 78752

Northwood Institute
Hotel and Restaurant
Management
Farm Road 1382
Cedar Hill, TX 75104-0058

San Jacinto College—North
Campus
Chef's Training
5800 Uvaldo
Houston, TX 77049

South Plains College—Lubbock
Food Industry Management
1302 Main Street
Lubbock, TX 79401

St. Phillip's College
Hospitality Operations
2111 Nevada
San Antonio, TX 78203

Texas State Technical Institute
Foodservice Technology
3801 Campus Drive
Waco, TX 76705

Utah

Dixie College
Hotel and Restaurant
Management Program
St. George, UT 84770

Sevier Valley Tech
Foodservices/Cooking
800 West 200 South
Richfield, UT 84701

Utah Valley Community College
  Hotel, Motel, Restaurant
    Management
  800 W. 1200 S.
  Orem, UT 84058

Vermont

Champlain College
  Hotel, Restaurant Management
  P.O. Box 670
  Burlington, VT 05402

New England Culinary Institute
  Culinary Arts
  250 Main Street
  Montpelier, VT 05602

Virginia

J. Sargeant Reynolds
    Community College
  Hotel and Restaurant
    Management Program
  P.O. Box 85622
  Richmond, VA 23285

National Business College
  Hotel and Restaurant
    Management Program
  P.O. Box 6400
  Roanoke, VA 24017

Thomas Nelson Community
    College
  Hotel, Restaurant and
    Institutional Management
  P.O. Box 9407
  Hampton, VA 23670

Northern Virginia Community
    College
  Hotel, Restaurant and
    Institutional Management
  8333 Little River Turnpike
  Annandale, VA 22003

Tidewater Community College
  Hotel, Restaurant and
    Institutional Management
  1700 College Crescent
  Virginia Beach, VA 23456

Washington

Clark Community College
  Culinary Arts/Restaurant
    Management
  1800 E. McLoughlin
    Boulevard
  Vancouver, WA 98663

Edmonds Community
    College
  Culinary Arts
  20000 68th Avenue West
  Lynnwood, WA 98036

Everett Community College
  Food Technology
  801 Wetmore Avenue
  Everett, WA 98201

Highline Community College
  Hospitality and Tourism
    Management
  P.O. Box 98000
  Des Moines, WA 98198-9800

Lake Washington Technical
    College
  Hotel and Restaurant
    Management Program
  Kirkland, WA 98034

North Seattle Community
    College
  Hospitality and Foodservice/
    Culinary Arts
  9600 College Way North
  Seattle, WA 98103

Olympic College
  Foodservice Program
  16th & Chester
  Bremerton, WA 98310

Pierce College
  Foodservice Management
  9401 Far West Drive S.W.
  Fort Lewis, WA 98433

Renton Vocational Technical
    Institute
  Culinary Arts
  3000 N.E. Fourth Street
  Renton, WA 98056

Seattle Central Community
    College
  Hospitality/Culinary Arts
  1701 Broadway, M/S 2120
  Seattle, WA 98122

Skagit Valley College
  Foodservice Hospitality
  2405 College Way
  Mount Vernon, WA 98273

South Seattle Community College
  Culinary Arts
  6000 16th Avenue S.W.
  Seattle, WA 98106

Spokane Community College
  Hotel, Motel, Restaurant
    Management
  N. 1810 Greene Street
  Spokane, WA 99207

Yakima Valley Community
    College
  Hotel and Restaurant
    Management Program
  P.O. Box 1647
  Yakima, WA 98907

West Virginia

Community College of West
    Virginia State
    Hospitality Management
    Campus Box 183
    Institute, WV 25112

Fairmont State College
    Foodservice Management
    Locust Avenue
    Fairmont, WV 26554

Garnet Career Center
    Foodservice and Hospitality
    422 Dickinson Street
    Charleston, WV 25314

James Rumsey Vocational
    Technical Center
    Culinary Arts
    Route 6, Box 268
    Martinsburg, WV 25401

Shepherd College
    Hotel, Motel and Restaurant
    Management
    King Street
    Shepherdstown, WV 25401

Wisconsin

Chippewa Valley Technical
    College
    Restaurant and Hotel Cookery/
    Hospitality Management
    620 W. Clairemont Avenue
    Eau Claire, WI 54701

Fox Valley Technical College
    Restaurant and Hotel
    Management and Cookery
    1825 N. Bluemound Drive
    Appleton, WI 54913

Gateway Technical College
    Hotel, Motel Management
    1001 S. Main Street
    Racine, WI 53403

Madison Area Technical College
    Culinary Trades
    3550 Anderson Street
    Madison, WI 53704

Mid-State Technical College
    Food and Hospitality
    Management
    500 32nd Street North
    Wisconsin Rapids, WI 54494

Milwaukee Area Technical
    College
    Restaurant and Hotel Cookery
    700 W. State Street
    Milwaukee, WI 53233

Moraine Park Technical College
    Restaurant and Hotel Cookery
    235 N. National Avenue
    Fond du Lack, WI 54935

Nicolet Area Technical College
    Hospitality Management/
    Food Preparation
    P.O. Box 518
    Rhinelander, WI 54501

Southwest Wisconsin Technical
College
Foodservice Management
Highway 18 East
Fennimore, WI 53809

Waukesha County Technical
College
Hospitality Management/
Culinary Arts
800 Main Street
Pewaukee, WI 53072

Western Wisconsin Technical
College
Foodservice Management
6th and Vine
La Crosse, WI 54601

Wisconsin Indianhead Technical
College
Hospitality Management
2100 Beaser Avenue
Ashland, WI 54806

Wyoming

Laramie County Community
College
Hotel and Restaurant
Management Program
Cheyenne, WY 82007

FOUR-YEAR SCHOOL PROGRAMS IN HOTEL, RESTAURANT, AND INSTITUTIONAL MANAGEMENT

The following list is arranged alphabetically by state. Additional information for most schools listed are available directly from the school, including: number of students enrolled; number of faculty; names of directors of programs; costs; and brief program descriptions.

Contact each school for additional information on its program. Programs marked with an (M) indicate that the school offers a master's degree program.

Alabama

Auburn University
Hotel, Restaurant
Management Program
School of Human Sciences
328 Spidle Hall
Auburn, AL 36849-5605

Tuskegee University
Hospitality Management
Program
Department of Home
Economics
Tuskegee, AL 36088

University of Alabama
Restaurant and Hospitality
Management Program
College of Human
Environmental Sciences
P.O. Box 870158
Tuscaloosa, AL 35487

Alaska

Alaska Pacific University
Travel and Hospitality
Management
School of Management
4101 University Drive
Anchorage, AK 99508

University of Alaska
Travel Industry Management
Program
School of Management
Fairbanks, AK 99709

Arizona

Northern Arizona University
School of Hotel and Restaurant
Management
NAU Box 5638
Flagstaff, AZ 86011

Arkansas

Arkansas Tech University
Hotel and Restaurant
Management
School of Business
Corley Building
Russellville, AR 72801

University of Arkansas
at Pine Bluff
Foodservice, Restaurant
Management
Home Economics Department
P.O. Box 4128
Pine Bluff, AR 71601

California

California State Polytechnic
University
Center for Hospitality
Management
3801 W. Temple Avenue
Pomona, CA 91768

California State University, Chico
Foodservice Administration
School of Home Economics
117 Glenn Hall
Chico, CA 95929-0002

California State University,
Long Beach
Food Administration
Department of Home
Economics
1250 Bellflower Boulevard
Long Beach, CA 90840

Chapman College
Hotel, Restaurant and Tourism
Management
Orange, CA 92666

Golden Gate University (M)
    Hotel, Restaurant and Tourism
        Management
    College of Business
        Administration
    536 Mission Street
    San Francisco, CA 94105

Loma Linda University
    Food Systems Management
    Department of Nutrition and
        Dietetics
    Loma Linda, CA 92354

San Jose State University
    Foodservice Management
    Department of Nutrition and
        Food Science
    One Washington Square
    San Jose, CA 95192

United States International
        University
    School of Hospitality
        Management
    10455 Pomerado Road
    San Diego, CA 92131

University of San Francisco
    Hospitality Management
    School of Business
    Ignatian Heights
    San Francisco, CA 94117

Colorado

Colorado State University
    Restaurant Management
    Department of Food Sciences
        and Human Nutrition
    Fort Collins, CO 80523

Metropolitan State College
    Hospitality, Meeting, Travel
        Administration
    1006 11th Street—Box 60
    Denver, CO 80204

University of Denver
    School of Hotel and Restaurant
        Management
    2030 E. Evans Avenue
    Denver, CO 80208

Connecticut

University of New Haven (M)
    School of Hotel, Restaurant
        and Tourism Administration
    300 Orange Avenue
    West Haven, CT 06516

Delaware

Delaware State College
Hotel and Restaurant
Management
Department of Home
Economics
1200 DuPont Highway
Dover, DE 19901

University of Delaware
Hotel, Restaurant and
Institutional Management
College of Human Resources
Alison Hall
Newark, DE 19716

District of Columbia

Howard University
Hotel, Motel Management
School of Business
2600 6th Street NW
Washington, DC 20059

Florida

Bethune-Cookman College
Hospitality Management
Program
Division of Business
640 Second Avenue
Daytona Beach, FL 32115

College of Boca Raton
Hotel, Restaurant and Tourism
Management
3601 N. Military Trail
Boca Raton, FL 33431

Florida International University
(M)
School of Hospitality
Management
15101 Biscayne
Boulevard
North Miami, FL 33181

Florida Southern College
Hotel and Restaurant
Management Program
Lakeland, FL 33801

Lynn University
Hotel and Restaurant
Management Program
Boca Raton, FL 33431

Florida State University
Hospitality Administration
School of Business
225 William Johnston Building
Tallahassee, FL 32306

Saint Leo College
Restaurant and Hotel
Management
State Road 52,
P.O. Box 2067
Saint Leo, FL 33574

St. Thomas University
Tourism and Hospitality
Management
School of Business,
Economics, Sports and Tourism
16400 NW 32nd Avenue
Miami, FL 33138

Schiller International University
 Hotel and Restaurant
  Management Program
 Dunedin, FL 34698

University of Central Florida
 Hospitality Management
  Department
 College of Business
 CEBA II #409
 Orlando, FL 32816

Webber College
 Hotel and Restaurant
  Management
 1201 Alternate Highway
  27 South
 Babson Park, FL 33827

Georgia

Clark Atlanta University
 Hotel and Restaurant
  Management Program
 James B. Brawley Drive
  at Fair Street
 Atlanta, GA 30314

Georgia Southern University
 Restaurant, Hotel, and
  Institutional Administration
 Division of Home Economics
 Landrum Box 8034
 Statesboro, GA 30458

Georgia State University
 Hotel, Restaurant and Travel
  Administration
 College of Public and
  Urban Affairs
 University Plaza
 Atlanta, GA 30303

Morris Brown College
 Hospitality Administration
 643 Martin Luther King Drive
 Atlanta, GA 30314

University of Georgia
 Hotel and Restaurant
  Administration
 College of Home Economics
 Dawson Hall
 Athens, GA 30602

Hawaii

Brigham Young University—
Hawaii
Hospitality Management
Business Division
55-220 Kulanui
Laie, HI 96762

Hawaii Pacific College
Travel Industry Management
1188 Fort Street
Honolulu, HI 96813

University of Hawaii—Manoa
School of Travel Industry
Management
2560 Campus Road,
George Hall
Honolulu, HI 96822

Illinois

Chicago State University
Hotel and Restaurant
Management
College of Business and
Administration
95th Street at King Drive
Chicago, IL 60628

Eastern Illinois University
Hospitality Services
Program
School of Home
Economics
109 Klehm Hall,
S.H.E.
Charleston, IL 61920

Kendall College
Hospitality Management
2408 Orrington Avenue
Evanston, IL 60201

Northern Illinois University
Food Science
Department of Human and
Family Resources
DeKalb, IL 60115

Roosevelt University
Hospitality Management
430 S. Michigan Avenue
Chicago, IL 60605

Southern Illinois University
Food and Lodging Systems
Management
College of Agriculture
Quigley Hall, Room 209
Carbondale, IL 62901

University of Illinois (M)
Hospitality Management
School of Human Resources
and Family Studies
363 Bevier Hall,
905 S. Goodwin Avenue
Urbana, IL 61801

Western Illinois University
Foodservice and Lodging
Management Program
Department of Home
Economics
204 Knoblauch Hall
Macomb, IL 61455

Indiana

Ball State University
  Foodservice Management
  Home Economics Department
  Practical Arts Building
  Muncie, IN 47306

Purdue University Calumet
  Hotel and Restaurant
    Management Program
  173rd and Woodmar Avenue
  Hammond, IN 46323

Purdue University (M)
  Department of Restaurant,
    Hotel and Institutional
    Management
  School of Consumer and
    Family Sciences
  106 Stone Hall
  West Lafayette, IN 47907

Iowa

Iowa State University (M)
  Hotel, Restaurant, and
    Institutional Management
  College of Family and
    Consumer Sciences
  11 MacKay Hall
  Ames, IA 50011

Kansas

Kansas State University
  Hotel and Restaurant
    Management
  College of Human Ecology
  Justin Hall
  Manhattan, KS 66506

Kentucky

Berea College
  Hotel and Restaurant
    Management
    Program
  CPO 2344
  Berea, KY 40404

Morehead State University
  Hotel, Restaurant and
    Institutional Management
  Department of Home
    Economics
  UPO Box 889
  Morehead, KY 40351

Transylvania University
  Hotel, Restaurant, and Tourism
    Administration
  Division of Business
    Administration
  300 N. Broadway
  Lexington, KY 40508

University of Kentucky
  Restaurant Management
  College of Home Economics
  210 Erikson Hall
  Lexington, KY 40506

Western Kentucky University
  Hotel, Motel, Restaurant
    Management
  Department of Home
    Economics and
    Family Living
  Academic Complex
  Bowling Green, KY 42101

Louisiana

Grambling State University
  Hotel and Restaurant
    Management
  P.O. Box 882
  Grambling, LA 61245

University of New Orleans
  School of Hotel, Restaurant
    and Tourism Administration
  College of Business
  New Orleans, LA 70148

University of Southwestern
    Louisiana
  Restaurant Administration
  School of Home Economics
  USL P.O. Box 40399,
    200 E. University
  Lafayette, LA 70504

Maine

Thomas College
  Hotel and Restaurant
    Management Program
  Waterville, ME 04901

University of Maine at Machias
  Hotel and Restaurant
    Management Program
  Machias, ME 04654

Maryland

Morgan State University
Hotel and Restaurant
Management Program
Cold Spring Lane and
Hillen Road
Baltimore, MD 21251

University of Maryland
Food Systems
College of Human Ecology
College Park, MD 20742

University of Maryland–
Eastern Shore
Hotel and Restaurant
Management
School of Professional Studies
Somerset Hall, Room 409
Princess Anne, MD 21853

Massachusetts

Boston University
Hotel and Food Administration
Metropolitan College
808 Commonwealth Avenue
Boston, MA 02215

Framingham State College
Foodservice Systems
Management
Department of Home
Economics
State Street, Hemenway Hall
Framingham, MA 01701

Lasell College
Hotel and Restaurant
Management Program
Newton, MA 02166

Mount Ida College
Hotel and Restaurant
Management Program
Newton Centre, MA 02159

University of Massachusetts (M)
Department of Hotel,
Restaurant and Travel
Administration
College of Food and
Natural Resources
Flint Laboratory, Room 107
Amherst, MA 01003

Michigan

Central Michigan University
Marketing and Hospitality
Services Administration
College of Business
100 Smith Hall
Mt. Pleasant, MI 48859

Davenport College of Business
Restaurant and Lodging
Management Program
415 E. Fulton
Grand Rapids, MI 49507

Eastern Michigan
  University
  Hospitality
    Management
  Human Environmental and
    Consumer Resources
  202 Roosevelt Hall
  Ypsilanti, MI 48197

Ferris State University
  Hospitality
    Management
  School of Business
  901 S. State Street
  Big Rapids, MI 49307

Grand Valley State
  University
  Hospitality and Tourism
    Management
  Science and Mathematics
    Division
  AuSable 111
  Allendale, MI 49401

Michigan State University (M)
  School of Hotel, Restaurant
    and Institutional
    Management
  425 Eppley Center
  East Lansing, MI 48824-1121

Northern Michigan University
  Restaurant and Foodservice
    Management
  School of Technology and
    Applied Science
  Jacobetti Center, Route 550
  Marquette, MI 49855

Northwood University
  Hotel and Restaurant
    Management Program
  Midland, MI 48640

Siena Heights College
  Hotel, Restaurant and
    Institutional Management
  1247 E. Siena Heights Drive
  Adrian, MI 49221

Minnesota

Mankato State University
  Food and Nutrition
  Home Economics
    Department
  P.O. Box 9400, MSU Box 44
  Mankato, MN 56002-8400

Moorhead State University
  Hotel, Motel, Restaurant
    Management
  Department of Business
    Administration
  Moorhead, MN 56560

Southwest State University
  Hotel and Restaurant
    Administration Program
  Department of Hospitality,
    Marketing, and
    Agribusiness
  Lecture Center 101
  Marshall, MN 56285

University of Minnesota,
  Crookston
  Hotel and Restaurant
    Management Program
  Crookston, MN 56716

Mississippi

University of Southern
    Mississippi
    Hotel, Restaurant and Tourism
    Management
    College of Health and Human
    Sciences
S.S. Box 5035
Hattiesburg, MS 39406

Missouri

Central Missouri State University
    Hotel and Restaurant
    Administration
    Home Economics Department
    Grinstead 250
    Warrensburg, MO 64093

College of the Ozarks
    Hotel and Restaurant
    Management Program
    Point Lookout, MO 65726

Southwest Missouri State
    University
    Hospitality and Restaurant
    Administration
    College of Health and
    Applied Science
    901 S. National
    Springfield, MO 65804

University of Missouri
    Hotel and Restaurant
    Management Program
    Department of Food Science
    and Nutrition
    122 Eckles Hall
    Columbia, MO 65211

Nebraska

University of Nebraska
    Foodservice Management
    Department of Home
    Economics
    316 Ruth Leverton
    Lincoln, NE 68583

University of Nebraska
    Restaurant Management
    School of Human Nutrition
    60th and Dodge
    Omaha, NE 68182-0214

Nevada

Sierra Nevada College—
Lake Tahoe
Hotel, Restaurant and Resort
Management
P.O. Box 4269, 800 College
Drive
Incline Village, NV 89450

University of Nevada—
Las Vegas (M)
College of Hotel
Administration
4505 Maryland Parkway
Las Vegas, NV 89154-6013

New Hampshire

New Hampshire College
Hotel, Restaurant
Management and
Culinary Arts
2500 N. River Road
Manchester, NH 03104

University of New Hampshire
Hotel Administration
School of Business
and Economics
McConnell Hall
Durham, NH 03824

New Jersey

Fairleigh Dickinson University (M)
School of Hotel, Restaurant,
and Tourism Management
Hesslein Building
Rutherford, NJ 07070

Montclair State College
Foodservice Management
Home Economics Department
Upper Montclair, NJ 07043

Thomas Edison State College
Hotel and Restaurant
Management Program
101 W. State Street
Trenton, NJ 08608

New Mexico

New Mexico State University
Hospitality and Tourism
Services Program
College of Agriculture and
Home Economics
P.O. Box 30003,
Department 3HTS
Las Cruces, NM 88003

New York

Buffalo State College
Food Systems Management
Nutrition and Food Science
Department
1300 Elmwood Avenue,
Caudell 106
Buffalo, NY 14222

Canisius College
Hotel and Restaurant
Management Program
2001 Main Street
Buffalo, NY 14208

City University of New York
Hotel and Restaurant
Management Department
New York City
Technical College
300 Jay Street
Brooklyn, NY 11201

Cornell University (M)
School of Hotel
Administration
Statler Hall
Ithaca, NY 14853

Keuka College
Hotel and Restaurant
Management Program
Keuka Park, NY 14478

Marymount College
Foods for Business
and Industry
Department of Human
Ecology
Box 1375
Tarrytown, NY 10591

New York Institute of Technology
School of Hotel, Restaurant
Administration
Northern Boulevard
Old Westbury, NY 11568-9998

New York University (M)
Center for Food and Hotel
Management
East Building, Room 537
239 Greene Street
New York, NY 10003

Niagara University
Institute of Travel, Hotel and
Restaurant Administration
Niagara University, NY 14109

Rochester Institute of
Technology (M)
School of Food, Hotel,
Tourism Management
1 Lomb Memorial Drive,
P.O. Box 9887
Rochester, NY 14623

State University of New York
at Oneonta
Food and Business
Department of Home
Economics
Oneonta, NY 13820-4015

State University of New York
at Plattsburgh
Hotel and Restaurant
Management
Center for Human Resources
Draper AVenue, Ward Hall
Plattsburgh, NY 12901

Syracuse University
　Food Systems Management
　College for Human
　　Development
　112 Slocum Hall
　Syracuse, NY 13244

North Carolina

Appalachian State University
　Hospitality Management
　　Program
　College of Business
　Boone, NC 28608

Barber-Scotia College
　Hotel, Restaurant Management
　145 Cabanus Avenue W.
　Concord, NC 28025

East Carolina University
　Hospitality Management
　School of Home Economics

Greenville, NC 27858

North Carolina Central University
　Institutional Management
　Department of Home
　　Economics
　P.O. Box 19615
　Durham, NC 27707

North Carolina Wesleyan College
　Foodservice and Hotel
　　Management
　Wesleyan Station
　Rocky Mount, NC 27803

North Dakota

North Dakota State University
　Hotel, Motel and Restaurant
　　Management
　College of Home Economics
　Fargo, NC 58105

Ohio

Ashland University
　Hotel, Restaurant
　　Program
　School of Business
　401 College Avenue
　Ashland, OH 44805

Bowling Green State University
　Restaurant and Institutional
　　Foodservice Management
　Department of Applied
　　Human Ecology
　106 Johnston Hall
　Bowling Green, OH
　　43403-0254

Central State University
  Hotel and Restaurant
    Management Program
  Wilberforce, OH 45384

Kent State University
  Hospitality Foodservice
    Management
  School of Family and
    Consumer Studies
  103 Nixson Hall
  Kent, OH 44242

Ohio State University
  Hospitality Management
  College of Human Ecology
  1787 Neil Avenue, 265
  Campbell Hall
  Columbus, OH 43210

Tiffin University
  Hotel and Restaurant
    Management
  155 Miami Street
  Tiffin, OH 44883

Youngstown State University
  Hotel and Restaurant
    Management Program
  One University Plaza
  Youngstown, OH 44555

Oklahoma

Langston University
  Hospitality Management
  Division of Business
  P.O. Box 339
  Langston, OK 73050

Oklahoma State University
  School of Hotel and Restaurant
    Administration
  College of Home Economics
  210 Home Economics West
  Stillwater, OK 74078

University of Central Oklahoma
  Hotel and Restaurant
    Management Program
  Edmund, OK 73034

Oregon

Oregon State University
  Hotel, Restaurant and Tourism
    Management
  College of Business
  Bexell Hall, Room 201
  Corvallis, OR 97331-2603

Southern Oregon University
  Hotel and Restaurant
    Management Program
  Ashland, OR 97520

Pennsylvania

Cheyney University
  Hotel, Restaurant and
    Institutional Management
  Cheyney, PA 19319

Drexel University
  Hotel, Restaurant and
    Institutional Management
  College of Design Arts
  33rd and Market Street
  Philadelphia, PA 19104

East Stroudsburg University
  Hospitality Management
  School of Professional Studies
  Hospitality Management
    Center
  East Stroudsburg, PA 18301

Indiana University of
    Pennsylvania
  Hotel, Restaurant, and
    Institutional Management
  Human Ecology and Health
    Sciences
  Ackerman Hall
  Indiana, PA 15701

Lebanon Valley College
  Hotel and Restaurant
    Management Program
  Annville, PA 17003

Marywood College
  Hotel and Restaurant
    Management
  2300 Adams Avenue
  Scranton, PA 18509-1598

Mercyhurst College
  Hotel, Restaurant and
    Institutional Management
  Glenwood Hills
  Erie, PA 16546

Pennsylvania State University
    (M)
  School of Hotel, Restaurant
    and Institutional
    Management
  118 Henderson Building
  University Park, PA 16802

Widener University
  School of Hotel and Restaurant
    Management
  17th Street
  Chester, PA 19013

Rhode Island

Johnson & Wales University (M)
  Hospitality Department
  Business Division
  8 Abbott Park Place
  Providence, RI 02903

South Carolina

Johnson and Wales University
Hotel and Restaurant
Management Program
PCC Box 14G9
701 E. Bay Street
Charleston, SC 29403

University of South Carolina
Hotel, Restaurant and Tourism
Administration
College of Applied
Professional Sciences
Columbia, SC 29208

Winthrop College
Food Systems Management
Department of Human
Nutrition
103 Crawford Health Center
Rock Hill, SC 29733

South Dakota

Black Hills State University
Travel Industry Management
College of Business and
Public Affairs
1200 University
Spearfish, SD 57783

Huron University
Hotel and Restaurant
Management
Business Department
8th and Ohio
Huron, SD 57350

South Dakota State University
Restaurant Management
College of Home Economics
P.O. Box 2275A SDSU
Brookings, SD 57007

Tennessee

Belmont University
Hospitality Business
1900 Belmont
Boulevard
Nashville, TN 37212

Tennessee State University
Foodservice Management
Department of Home
Economics
3500 John Merritt Boulevard
Nashville, TN 37209

University of Tennessee
Hotel and Restaurant
Administration
College of Human Ecology
229 Jessie Harris Building
Knoxville, TN 37996-1900

Texas

Huston-Tillotson College
Hotel and Restaurant
Management
1820 E. 8th Street
Austin, TX 78702

Lamar University
Restaurant and Institutional
Food Management
School of Education
P.O. Box 10035
Beaumont, TX 77710

Texas A&M University,
Kingsville
Hotel and Restaurant
Management Program
Kingsville, TX 78363

Texas Tech University (M)
Restaurant, Hotel and
Institutional Management
College of Home Economics
Box 4170
Lubbock, TX 79409

Texas Woman's University
Institutional Administration
Department of Nutrition and
Food Sciences
P.O. Box 24134, TWU Station
Denton, TX 76204

University of Houston (M)
College of Hotel and
Restaurant Management
Houston, TX 77204-3902

University of the Incarnate Word
Hotel and Restaurant
Management Program
4301 Broadway
San Antonio, TX 78209

University of North Texas (M)
Hotel and Restaurant
Management
School of Human Resource
Management
P.O. Box 5248
Denton, TX 76203

Wiley College
Hotel and Restaurant
Management
711 Wiley Avenue
Marshall, TX 75670

Vermont

Champlain College
  Hotel and Restaurant
    Management Program
  163 S. Willard Street
  Burlington, VT 05401

Johnson State College
  Hotel, Hospitality
    Management
  Johnson, VT 05656

New England Culinary Institute
  Food Service Management
  Montpelier, VT 05602

Southern Vermont College
  Hotel and Restaurant
    Management Program
  Bennington, VT 05201

Vermont College of Norwich
    University
  Hotel Administration Program
  Montpelier, VT 05602

Virginia

Hampton University
  Hotel and Restaurant
    Management Program
  Hampton, VA 23668

Liberty University
  Foodservice Management
  Department of Human Ecology
  Box 20000
  Lynchburg, VA 24506-8001

James Madison University
  Hotel, Restaurant Management
  College of Business
  102 Harrison Hall
  Harrisonburg, VA 22807

Norfolk State University
  Hotel, Restaurant and
    Institutional Management
  School of Consumer Services
    and Family Studies
  2401 Corprew Avenue
  Norfolk, VA 23504

Radford University
  Restaurant Management
  Department of Health Service
  Norwood Street, Box 5826
  Radford, VA 24142

Virginia Polytechnic Institute and
    State University (M)
  Hotel, Restaurant and
    Institutional Management
  College of Human Resources
  18 Hillcrest Hall
  Blacksburg, VA 24061-0429

Virginia State University
  Hotel Restaurant Management
  College of Agriculture and
    Applied Sciences
  Box 427 HRM
  Petersburg, VA 23803

Washington

Washington State University
  Hotel and Restaurant
    Administration
  College of Business and
    Economics
  1108 E. Columbia
  Seattle, WA 98122

Washington State University
  Hotel and Restaurant
    Administration Program
  College of Business and
    Economics
  Todd Hall 245D
  Pullman, WA 99164-4724

West Virginia

Concord College
  Travel Industry Management
  Box 67
  Athens, WV 24712

Shepherd College
  Hotel, Motel, Restaurant
    Management
  Shepherdstown, WV 25401

University of Charleston
  Hotel and Restaurant
    Management Program
  2300 MacCorkle Avenue, S.E.
  Charleston, WV 25304

Wisconsin

Mount Mary College
  Hotel and Restaurant
    Management Program
  Milwaukee, WI 53222

University of Wisconsin—
    Madison
  Foodservice Administration
  College of Agricultural and
    Life Sciences
  1605 Linden Drive
  Madison, WI 53706

University of Wisconsin—
    Stevens Point
  Food Systems Administration
  School of Home Economics
  CPS Building
  Stevens Point, WI 54481

University of Wisconsin—Stout
  Hotel and Restaurant
    Management
  School of Home Economics
  Home Economics Building,
    Room 220
  Menomonie, WI 54751